Antonio Jain

Emotional Dependency, the Complete Guide

How to Break the Chains of Codependency, Eliminate
Relationship Anxiety and Achieve Your Freedom

This book is intended solely to provide general information and should not be considered legal, financial, medical or professional advice of any kind. The content of this book is provided for educational and informational purposes only and does not guarantee the accuracy, completeness or applicability of the information presented.

The author and publisher are not responsible for any action taken by the reader based on the information contained in this book. Readers are advised to consult appropriate professionals before making decisions or acting upon the information presented in this book.

The author and publisher of this book have made reasonable efforts to ensure the accuracy and reliability of the information provided in this book. However, neither the accuracy nor the completeness of the information contained in this book is guaranteed. The author and publisher assume no responsibility for any errors or omissions in the contents, as well as for any loss, damage, or injury that may result from the use of the information in this book.

All trademarks, service marks, trade names, product names, and logos appearing in this book are the property of their respective owners. The use of such trademarks, service marks, trade names, product names, and logos does not imply any affiliation, sponsorship, endorsement, or affiliation with the author and publisher of this book. The trademark holders assume no responsibility for the contents of this book.

Dear reader, you can win an Amazon gift certificate by leaving your opinion about this book through the following QR code, or by using this link:

https://bit.ly/antoniojaimezus-9

Preface: Beginning the Journey: Understanding Emotional Dependency

Hi! I'm Antonio Jaimez, and I'm really excited that you have embarked on this important journey with me. Your decision to explore this book indicates a courage and a willingness to commit to your personal growth that is truly worthy of admiration. I am grateful that you have chosen my work to help you on this path to self-understanding and emotional liberation.

For many years, I have dedicated my professional life to unraveling the complexities of the human heart, and especially, to understanding the ways in which emotional dependency can limit our potential and affect our relationships. I am pleased that you rely on my experience and expertise to support you in this challenge.

Your decision to open this book was a wise and informed one. Just as the decision to attend music school can help you master an instrument, or college can give you the skills you need to succeed in a career, this choice will provide you with valuable tools and techniques to manage your emotional life and improve your relationships.

A journey of discovery and personal growth awaits us. Throughout the chapters of this book, we will explore the origins of emotional dependency and how it can manifest itself in our lives. We will discuss self-esteem, the importance of self-care, and how assertiveness can help us express our needs without fear. I will share with you techniques to develop resilience and also stories of success and overcoming that, I am sure, will inspire you on your own journey.

It is my hope that this book will offer you the tools and inspiration you need to break your own emotional chains. The road may be challenging, but I promise you that the journey will be worth it. In the end, you will be able to enjoy the emotional benefits of a more independent, autonomous and fulfilling life.

But remember, this is not a book to read and forget. It is a manual, a guide to refer to when the going gets tough. I urge you to take your time, to reflect on what you have read, and to apply what you learn in your daily life. In doing so, I am convinced that you will find a new way of living and relating to others.

I am honored to be your guide on this journey. No matter how dark the road, there is always a light at the end of the tunnel. I am here to help you find it. Now, let's begin the journey.

With all my respect and appreciation,

Antonio Jaimez

Chapter 1: The Root of the Problem: Exploring the Origins of Emotional Dependence

Have you ever stopped to think about the foundations of a building? Those subway and hidden pillars that support all the weight of the structure. The stability of the building depends, to a great extent, on the solidity of these foundations. Likewise, to understand the phenomenon of emotional dependency, we must first dig down and examine its foundations, its roots.

Why is that? You may ask. Here is a popular saying that may clarify your doubts: "Knowing the origin of a problem is half the solution". We could not agree more with this ancient wisdom. Only by understanding where this dependency arises from can we begin to counteract it, soften its impact and, finally, free ourselves from its chains.

Emotional dependence has deep roots, often buried in our childhood and adolescent experiences. Early interactions with our caregivers, friends and family play a crucial role in shaping our adult relationships. Psychologists have explored this phenomenon for decades, building theories and models to explain it.

John Bowlby, an influential British psychologist, developed attachment theory in the mid-20th century, suggesting that relationship patterns established during our childhood may persist into our adult lives. His work "Attachment and Loss" (1969) is an inescapable reference for understanding how emotional dependence can be a manifestation of an insecure attachment established in the early years of life.

Early experiences can program, so to speak, our capacity to establish healthy relationships or, on the contrary, generate emotional dependencies. If we were to draw a map of emotional dependency, our childhood home would be located in the center. But, don't worry, this map is not carved in stone. You can redefine it. We are not condemned by our past, but if we want to free ourselves from these chains, we must first understand how they were formed.

Has it happened to you that you sometimes feel an irrational need for approval, affection or attention, to such an extent that you can't seem to control it? Or that your relationships seem to follow a painful pattern of dependency and anxiety, despite your best efforts to change? If so, this chapter will help you understand why this happens. Don't despair. Remember, understanding the problem is half the solution.

Well, now that we've opened the door to this theme, it's time to dive deeper into it. Are you ready to go beyond the surface? I promise you, the journey is worth it. After all, it's not every day you get the chance to become an archaeologist of your own mind. Here we go.

And remember, it's always better to laugh in life than to cry, isn't it? Now, let's continue our exploration.

In our childhood and adolescence, we absorb like sponges the attitudes and behaviors of those around us. But not only that, we are also molded by how they see and treat us. Social psychologist George Herbert Mead, in his work "Mind, Self, and Society" (1934), detailed how our identity is formed through social interactions. Our perception of ourselves often reflects how we believe others see us. Could you imagine how much this can influence the creation of emotional dependencies?

Following the metaphor of our building, early experiences form the foundation, but what about the walls and ceilings? What about the experiences and relationships we form during our adolescence and adulthood? Don't they also play a significant role in the formation of emotional dependency? The answer, of course, is a resounding yes.

To illustrate this, clinical psychologist Susan Forward in her book "Emotional Blackmail" (1997), addressed how emotional manipulations can create patterns of dependency. Often, these patterns can emerge without us even realizing it, until we find ourselves caught in a web of guilt and fear.

Fear, by the way, is a major player in the plot of emotional dependency. In her work "The Dance of Fear" (2005), psychotherapist Harriet Lerner talks about how fear can influence our relationships and how emotional dependence can be a way to avoid the fear of loneliness, rejection, or confrontation.

Do you identify with any of this? If so, I want you to know that you are not alone. We've all experienced fear in our relationships, and we've all had to struggle with patterns of behavior that are unhealthy. The first step toward liberation is recognizing that there is a problem and that it has a solution. And you know what? You have the power to solve it.

That said, it is essential to remember that understanding the origin of emotional dependency does not mean blaming anyone. Not your parents, not your friends, not society. And above all, not yourself. As Carl Jung, the Swiss psychiatrist and psychologist, said in his work "Psychology and Alchemy" (1953): "I do not agree that we are destined to repeat our past, I am convinced that we can learn from it". Understanding the origin of our emotional dependency is simply a tool for self-knowledge and personal growth.

As we get deeper into the root of the problem, painful emotions and memories are likely to emerge. I want you to know that it is okay to feel this way. We are here to face our shadows and heal. And remember, this is just the beginning of the journey - are you ready to keep exploring? Because there is still a lot of ground to cover and a lot of chains to break. Come on, let's get on with our exploration.

An excellent example of how emotional dependency can take shape in our lives is found in "Attached: The New Science of Adult Attachment and How It Can Help You Find-and Keep-Love" (2010). The authors, Amir Levine and Rachel Heller, explain how the attachment patterns we develop during our childhood can affect our adult relationships.

Imagine growing up in an environment where you are shown love and appreciation only when you behave in a certain way. It is likely that, as you grow up, you will find yourself desperately seeking approval from others in order to feel loved and valued. This behavior can lead to an emotionally dependent relationship in which you find yourself giving too much for too little.

Or think of those who grew up in homes where affection and attention were unpredictable, where one day they were the object of affection and the next day, indifference. These people may develop what is known as anxious attachment, which could lead to emotionally unstable relationships and a constant sense of insecurity.

Do any of these situations sound familiar? If so, let me remind you that you are not alone. Each of us carries baggage, and this book is the place where we go to get rid of what we don't need to carry with us.

In addition, it is important to understand that while these experiences may leave a deep impression, they do not completely determine who we are or what our relationships will be like. As Carl R. Rogers, humanistic psychologist, said in his work "On Becoming a Person" (1961): "What I am is good enough if I can become it". By this, I mean that you have the capacity to grow, change and free yourself from emotional dependency. Are you ready to move forward on this path to emotional freedom?

Now, I'm sure we've all heard the phrase "love is blind". In "The Betrayal Bond: Breaking Free of Exploitive Relationships" (1997), Patrick Carnes delves into this concept and shows how in some relationships, people can develop strong, destructive bonds, even when the relationship is harmful to them. It is as if they are tied to the person who hurts them. These are the chains of emotional dependency that we are seeking to break.

Remember, it is always better to ask questions than to remain ignorant. So I invite you to reflect: Have you ever experienced such a bond? Do you feel that you are in a relationship that hurts you, but that you can't get out of? If so, I want you to know that you are not alone and that there is a way out.

We are on this journey together and there is nothing you cannot overcome. As we move forward, I am convinced that you will find the tools and strength you need to throw off the chains of emotional dependency. I'm here to help you, and I'm excited to see the growth and transformation that is to come. Are you ready to move forward? Then let's move forward!

As we explore these deep roots, we also discover that the path to emotional liberation is a personal and intimate journey. This journey may involve recognizing patterns of behavior that may be difficult to confront. But keep in mind, dear reader, that the courage to face oneself is a testament to the human desire to grow and evolve.

Someone who reflects this beautifully is Brené Brown, a researcher and author, who in her book "The Gifts of Imperfection" (2010) talks about how our fears and vulnerabilities can be transformed into strengths. This is a lesson we can all take with us on our path to emotional freedom.

As we move forward on this journey, we must also remember the importance of self-acceptance. As Carl R. Rogers mentioned in his work "A Way of Being" (1980), "The curious paradox is that when I accept myself as I am, then I can change."

This wisdom underscores a key principle in our journey: emotional liberation begins with self-acceptance. Have you ever stopped to think about this? How would it feel to embrace all your parts, even those you consider less than perfect? Perhaps this could be the first step in freeing yourself from the chains of emotional dependency.

So what have we explored so far in this first chapter? We have come to understand that the roots of emotional dependency often lie in our early experiences, in how we are formed and how we experience love and acceptance in our lives.

We have also discovered that emotional dependency can take many forms, from toxic relationships to treacherous attachments. However, despite its complicated nature, emotional dependency is not a life sentence. On the contrary, with understanding, courage and acceptance, we can begin to throw off these chains.

So now that we've unraveled the root of the problem, it's time to dig a little deeper. In the next chapter, we'll delve into the fascinating world of self-esteem and its role in emotional dependency. We'll explore how healthy self-esteem can be a powerful tool for emotional release.

I assure you that this next journey will be eye-opening and provide you with tools to build a healthier and more autonomous relationship with yourself. Are you ready to continue on this exciting journey towards emotional freedom? If so, see you in the next chapter!

Chapter 2: The Role of Self-esteem in Emotional Dependence

Have you ever noticed how the strongest trees, with their roots deeply rooted in the earth, withstand even the most devastating storms? It is these trees that inspire us to stand firm in the midst of adversity. However, have you ever thought about what might happen if their bark weakens or their branches become brittle? Even with the strongest roots, the tree would be in danger.

Self-esteem can be compared to the bark of that tree, providing it with the strength and protection it needs to face the storms of life. Now, I invite you to reflect: How is your self-esteem? Is it strong and resilient, or has it perhaps weakened over time?

Recognizing the role of self-esteem in emotional dependence is a key piece of the puzzle we are solving. The relationship between these two concepts is like a dance in which each influences and shapes the other. With healthy self-esteem, we are able to establish balanced and satisfying relationships, where our value is not defined by others, but by ourselves. However, with low self-esteem, we can fall into the trap of emotional dependency, seeking in others what we are not able to give ourselves.

Nathaniel Branden, in his book "The Six Pillars of Self-Esteem" (1994), points out that "self-esteem is the experience of being competent to meet the basic challenges of life and being worthy of happiness." Now, tell me, isn't this competence and dignity what we often look for in others when we find ourselves entangled in the webs of emotional dependency?

We could say, then, that self-esteem is our personal armor. It protects us, keeps us safe and provides us with the strength we need to move forward in life with confidence and authenticity. But what happens if this armor is damaged or weakened?

Imagine that self-esteem is like a cup of coffee. If the cup is full, you can move and dance without spilling a drop. But if the cup is half empty and someone pushes you, the coffee spills. Is it the pusher's fault? Not necessarily. If your cup had been full, the coffee wouldn't have spilled. Likewise, if your self-esteem is strong and healthy, life's pushes, while they may unsettle you a bit, won't cause you to spill your emotions out of control.

It is important that we begin to see self-esteem not only as a protective shield, but also as a source of empowerment. Healthy self-esteem gives us the freedom to be who we are, to love ourselves and to make decisions that benefit us.

In the following parts of this journey, we will explore how to fill that cup of self-esteem to the brim, creating a resilient shield against emotional dependency.

Sit comfortably, take a deep breath and let's go into this labyrinth, hand in hand with some of the most influential thinkers of our time.

Carl Rogers, one of the most prominent psychologists of the 20th century, in his work "On Becoming a Person" (1961), put forward an idea that was revolutionary at the time. Rogers argued that each of us has an innate tendency to grow and develop toward our full potential, a process he called "self actualization." However, this process can be hindered by emotional dependency and low self-esteem. Imagine a tomato plant trying to grow in a dark closet. It has all the potential to become a strong and fruitful plant, but without sunlight, it will wither and die. In the same way, your most authentic self can be overshadowed by emotional dependency.

And so how is it that we end up in this dark closet? How is it that our self-esteem can become so low that we allow other people to define our worth? This is where the theory of Albert Bandura, another leading figure in psychology, known for his social learning theory, comes in. In his book "Self-Efficacy: The Exercise of Control" (1997), Bandura argues that we learn about ourselves through our interactions with others and the world around us. Now, think for a moment about the people who have been significant in your life. What have they taught you about yourself?

The reality is that we are all susceptible to outside influences. But the good news is that we can also learn to strengthen our self-esteem, reject negative perceptions and embrace our own worth and dignity.

You may be wondering how. Let me illustrate with a story. Once, an elderly man planted a small rose bush in his garden. Although it was skinny and looked fragile, the man cared for it lovingly. He talked to it, gave it the water it needed, and protected it from strong winds. Over time, that little rose bush grew into a lush, strong bush, blooming with the most beautiful roses every spring. In the same way, we can cultivate our self-esteem.

Right now you may feel like that rose bush in the beginning, skinny and fragile. But remember, change is possible. And as we move forward on this path to emotional independence, we will learn together how to care for our self-esteem, how to strengthen it and, ultimately, how to flourish.

As we move further into this exploration, let's take a closer look at how this process of cultivating self-esteem takes shape in reality. And in this case, I'd like you to consider yourself as the protagonist of your own story. Are you ready? Okay, let's go back to the story of the rose bush we mentioned earlier.

This rose bush, which was initially fragile, was able to flourish thanks to three fundamental factors: the love, attention and care it received from the gardener. Can you see the connection between this story and your life? You may feel like I'm playing games with you, but let me show you how this connects to your journey to emotional independence.

The love that the gardener showed to the rose bush is equivalent to the self-love that you must cultivate within yourself. Do you find it difficult to love yourself? Perhaps it is. But let me remind you of the words of psychologist Kristin Neff in her book "Self-Compassion: The Proven Power of Being Kind to Yourself" (2011), where she argues that self-love is not a luxury, but a necessity. And, like the rose bush, you grow with love.

The attention the gardener paid to the rose bush represents self-awareness, awareness of your needs, desires, dreams, fears and limitations. Do you remember the last time you really listened to yourself? As popular psychologist Brené Brown suggests in "The Gifts of Imperfection" (2010), the path to self-love and personal fulfillment begins with self-acceptance and self-awareness.

The care the gardener provided to the rose bush symbolizes self-care. The authority on positive psychology, Martin Seligman, emphasizes in his work "Authentic Happiness" (2002) that self-care is an essential part of overall well-being. Just as the rose bush needed water and protection, you also need to take care of your body, mind and emotions in order to flourish.

Become the gardener of your own life. Plant the seeds of self-love, pay attention to your needs and dreams, and take care of yourself in the best possible way. In doing so, you will not only strengthen your self-esteem, but also free yourself from the chains of emotional dependency.

Does it seem like a long and difficult journey? It certainly is. But the journey of a thousand miles begins with a single step, and you are taking that step right now. And remember, we will always be here with you, walking this road together, one step at a time.

Let's pause here. Take a deep breath and reflect. How do you feel now? Are you ready to move forward? I hope so, because the best is yet to come.

Chapter 3: Unraveling the Chains: The Psychology of Dependency

Allow me, dear reader, to invite you to embark on a journey of discovery through the labyrinth of the human mind. Our goal in this phase of the journey is to understand the subtleties and complexities of emotional dependency from a psychological perspective. Why? Well, as the great philosopher Socrates once said, "Know thyself." This maxim not only urges us to know our strengths and weaknesses, but also to understand our thoughts, emotions and behaviors, as well as the underlying forces that drive them.

Emotional dependency is not only an emotional problem, but also a psychological issue. This dependency originates and grows in our mind, and it can be very revealing and liberating to unravel the psychological mechanisms that feed this dependency. Are you ready to delve into the depths of your mind? Do you feel a bit like Alice in Wonderland, about to enter a new and mysterious world? That's natural, but remember that you are safe and you are not alone on this journey.

The American psychologist Abraham Maslow, in his famous theory of the hierarchy of needs, argued that all human beings have a number of fundamental needs, such as the needs for belonging and love. These needs, if unmet, can lead to feelings of loneliness, anxiety and even despair. Do you ever remember feeling an intense need to be loved and accepted? Have you ever felt a deep fear of loneliness and rejection? These are the feelings and emotions that can sow the seeds of emotional dependency.

But how is it possible that such a human and universal need can become a dependency trap? This is where the concepts of attachment and self-esteem come into play, two key elements in the psychology of emotional dependence. Attachment refers to the emotional bonds we establish with others, while self-esteem refers to how we value and perceive ourselves. Insecure attachment and low self-esteem can make us vulnerable to emotional dependence.

Imagine, for a moment, that you are a tightrope walker walking a tightrope. Attachment is the rope you lean on and self-esteem is your balance beam. If the rope is slack or if your balance bar is weak, you are likely to wobble and fall. In terms of emotional dependency, falling means becoming dependent on someone to meet your emotional needs and validate your self-esteem.

Sounds challenging, doesn't it? But the good news is that you're not doomed to fall. You can learn how to strengthen your balance beam, adjust your rope tension and ultimately walk the tightrope of life with confidence and balance. Ready to learn how? Keep going, brave explorer of self-knowledge, we're about to delve into even deeper territories of dependency psychology.

Renowned clinical psychologist and author, Lisa Firestone, in her book "Conquering Your Critical Inner Voice" (2002), provides valuable insights into how our own self-criticism can sabotage our self-esteem. Have you ever had a little voice in your head telling you that you're not enough, that you're not worthy of love and respect? That's your inner critical voice, and it can be a big obstacle on your path to emotional independence. But don't worry, you're not alone. We all have an inner critical voice, and with the help of self-exploration and self-compassion, we can learn to silence it.

Imagine, if you can, a little monster in your mind that is always ready to criticize and belittle you. What would it look like? Does it have a menacing face and a high-pitched voice? Or perhaps it is more of a shadowy, silent figure that whispers doubts and fears in your ear? Visualizing your inner critical voice as an entity separate from you can be a powerful step in gaining control over it. Are you ready to face your inner monster? Don't be afraid, I am here with you, and together we can defeat it.

In "The Art of Loving" (1956), the famous psychoanalyst Erich Fromm argues that love is not simply a passive feeling, but a skill that can be learned and developed. This applies to love for others as well as love for oneself. Have you ever thought of self-love as a skill? That's a pretty revolutionary concept, don't you think? But think about it, if self-love is a skill, then we can learn to love ourselves more and better. And the more we love ourselves, the less we rely on others to validate our self-worth.

But self-love is not the only skill we can learn to free ourselves from emotional dependency. We can also learn to set healthy boundaries, express our needs and emotions assertively, and cultivate healthy interpersonal relationships. Each of these skills is like a tool in your toolbox for emotional independence. And as we continue our journey, we will explore each of these tools in more depth. So, dear reader, are you ready to go ahead and learn more about the wonderful skills that await you on the road to emotional independence?

All right, here we go. Following the thread of our previous thought, let me introduce you to the idea of "object relations". The famous British psychologist and psychoanalyst, Donald Winnicott, in his work "Playing and Reality" (1971), proposed this idea to explain how our early relationships with our caregivers shape us emotionally. The experiences we have in these early relationships form the basis of how we see ourselves and how we relate to others.

Think of a young child playing with a favorite toy. As the child interacts with the toy, he forms a relationship with it, which in turn influences how he sees himself and how he relates to the world. In infancy, our favorite toys are often our first "objects" of love and attachment. Now, what would happen if that toy were suddenly snatched, lost or broken? The child would probably feel great distress, wouldn't he? This is an example of how the loss of an attachment object can lead to feelings of dependency and fear.

But here's the good news: just as we can form relationships of dependence, we can also learn to form relationships of independence. Remember, as Fromm said, love is a skill that can be learned and developed. And that includes self-love. If you can learn to love yourself unconditionally and trust your ability to meet your own emotional needs, then you can free yourself from the chains of emotional dependency.

Let me tell you the story of Ana, a former client of mine. Ana grew up in a family where love and attention were conditional. As a result, Ana developed a strong emotional dependency on her partners in her adult life. But through therapy, Ana learned to recognize and question her patterns of dependency. She learned to love herself, set healthy boundaries and cultivate more balanced relationships. Most importantly, Ana learned that she didn't need validation from others to feel worthy and loved.

Now, I'd like you to pause and reflect a bit. Do you recognize any patterns of emotional dependency in your own life? What would your life be like if you could break free from those patterns and live with greater emotional independence? Let me tell you: it would be liberating, it would be powerful, and above all, it would be profoundly transformative.

Are you excited about the idea? So am I. So come on, keep going, and together, we'll continue this exciting journey to emotional freedom. I'll be waiting for you in the next chapter, where we'll explore the disguises of dependency and learn how to identify toxic relationships. Are you ready? Here we go!

Now that we have explored the depths of emotional dependency, you have seen how intricate and complex it can be. In some ways, it's like a maze. You find yourself on one path, turn one way and find yourself at a dead end. You turn around and find yourself on another path. It's like a constant dance of search and discovery.

But what if I told you that every twist and turn and every dead end are opportunities to learn, to grow, and ultimately to break free? Sounds paradoxical, doesn't it? But that's how things work in life and in our psychology. Every challenge, every difficulty, offers us the opportunity to learn something new about ourselves.

Now, let me refer you to the work of Albert Ellis, "Rational Emotive Behavior Therapy" (REBT) of 1962. Ellis proposed that it is not the situations themselves that upset us, but our beliefs about them. When we change our beliefs, we change our emotional response. Isn't that powerful? If we can learn to see our patterns of emotional dependency as opportunities for growth rather than dead ends, then we are one step closer to emotional freedom.

You've done an amazing job on this chapter, you've made it this far, and I'm proud of you. Yes, of you. You have had the courage to go into the deepest recesses of human psychology, to face yourself and your patterns. It's not easy, but I know you can do it.

And here we come to the end of this chapter. But don't worry, it's not the end of the journey. In fact, it's just the beginning. In the next chapter, we'll explore the "Disguises of Dependency: Toxic Relationships and How to Identify Them." I promise it will be eye-opening and, I hope, liberating. I'm excited to continue this journey with you. Ready for the next step? Let's go for it! I promise you that you will not be alone in this. I will be with you, step by step, until you reach the goal. Come on, dear reader, our journey is just beginning.

Chapter 4: The Disguises of Dependency: Toxic Relationships and How to Identify Them

Welcome, dear reader, to this new chapter of our journey. Today, we are going to venture down a path that may be a bit turbulent, but promises deep and valuable insights. Are you ready to face the challenge and move forward? I know you are, I trust in you, in your ability to face what we are about to discover together.

I propose a game. Imagine you are at a masked ball. Everyone is wearing a costume, each one more elaborate and sophisticated than the last. At first, you can only see the masks, but over time, as you become more familiar with the people, you begin to see beyond the costumes. You become aware of the personalities behind the disguises, the fears, the insecurities, the dependencies. Sound familiar? Well, that's exactly how emotional dependency works.

Emotional dependency is disguised in many ways in our lives, and one of the most deceptive is through toxic relationships. As you'll recall from Chapter 2, self-esteem plays a key role in emotional dependency. Remember when we talked about how low self-esteem can lead us to develop dependent relationships? Well, here's where that all comes to life.

Toxic relationships are those in which we feel trapped, in which we feel we are giving more than we are receiving, in which we feel we are losing our identity, our wants and needs in favor of the other person's. They are relationships that consume us, that wear us down and make us feel like we are walking on glass. These are relationships that consume us, that wear us down and make us feel like we are walking on glass. Have you ever felt like this? Have you ever felt like you are in a relationship that is not doing you any good, but you can't or don't know how to get out of it? If so, you may be in a toxic relationship.

This chapter is important because toxic relationships are, unfortunately, more common than we would like to think. Many people find themselves in them without even realizing it, because the disguises of dependency can be very convincing. But don't worry, together we are going to learn how to look beyond the disguises and identify the signs of toxic relationships. We're going to learn how to protect ourselves and how to remove ourselves from situations that don't do us good.

To begin with, let's think about what a toxic relationship means. What characteristics do you think it has? What types of behaviors are usually present? I invite you to think about it for a moment before reading on. Make a list if you wish, it can be a very revealing exercise. And don't worry, there are no right or wrong answers, just your thoughts and experiences. Ready? Let's move on.

Excellent, we have already done a great job reflecting on and beginning to explore the traits of toxic relationships. Now, let's dig deeper into this topic with the help of some expert voices.

Psychologist and author Lisa Firestone (2012) in her book "Conquer Your Critical Inner Voice" talks about how our "critical inner voice" can influence our relationships and how it can lead us to form harmful attachments. Lisa argues that when that inner voice tells us that we are not enough, that we don't deserve love or that we won't be able to handle rejection, we become dependent on relationships to validate our worth.

This concept ties in with what we saw in Chapter 2, about the importance of self-esteem in emotional dependence, remember? This is one of those junction points we see on our journey. We notice how the pieces of the puzzle begin to fit together.

On the other hand, psychologist and professor Steven Stosny (2015) in his book "Love without Hurt" identifies the cycles of emotional abuse in toxic relationships. Stosny shows us that these relationships usually follow a pattern of idealization, devaluation and discarding, resulting in a devastating emotional roller coaster effect for the person who is trapped in this cycle.

Idealization, devaluation, discarding? Have you ever felt a relationship go through these stages? It is not easy to admit, but the first step to free ourselves from these patterns is to recognize them.

Renowned author and therapist John Gottman (1994) in his book "Why Marriages Succeed or Fail" also offers a valuable perspective on toxic relationships. Gottman talks about the "Four Horsemen of the Apocalypse" in a relationship: criticism, contempt, defensiveness and obstruction. According to Gottman, these four behaviors are clear indicators of a toxic and destructive relationship.

So now that we have seen what these experts tell us, I want to invite you to reflect again. Have you experienced any of these behaviors in your relationships? Do you recognize the patterns of idealization, belittling and dismissal? Have you heard the criticism, contempt, defensiveness and stonewalling?

I propose that we stop here for a moment. Not out of fear of what we might find, but out of respect for the depth of these discoveries. Feel free to take a breath, to reflect, to write down your thoughts. I await you here, with an open heart and a desire to continue our journey together towards understanding and emotional freedom.

We are back, ready to continue. Whether you took a breather or stayed here with me, I thank you. It's not easy to look these things in the face, but here you are. You are brave, and I am with you every step of the way.

Let's take this to a more concrete level, to see how these toxic behaviors can manifest in everyday life. Does this scenario sound familiar? You've had a long day and you're excited to share your experiences with your partner. When you tell him or her about your day, he or she interrupts you and starts talking about his or her own without showing you the slightest empathy. That, my friend, is a sign of a toxic relationship.

Or how about this: in an argument, your partner not only discredits your views, but insults and ridicules you. You feel small, and your feelings are dismissed as unimportant. There's no doubt you're in the midst of toxic behavior.

These are just examples, and as you may know, there are countless ways in which toxicity can invade our relationships.

But what if I told you that emotional dependence can take an even more subtle and deceptive form? Think about this situation: your partner insists that you spend all your free time with her, to the point that you gradually distance yourself from your friends and your own interests. At first, it may seem that your partner simply wants to be with you. But over time, you realize that your world has shrunk and that you are completely dependent on her for your happiness. This, dear reader, is an example of emotional dependency disguised as love.

Now, think about the well-known author and relationship expert, Dr. Robert Firestone (2002), in his book "The Fantasy Bond". He describes this type of relationship as a "fantasy bond," where people maintain the illusion of being fused with their partner to feel secure and avoid the pain of separation. Here, emotional dependence is disguised as intimacy.

As we move forward on our journey, we must keep in mind that emotional dependency can take many forms and present itself in ways that are not always obvious. But don't worry, I'm here to help you navigate through these sometimes murky waters.

At the end of the day, what matters is not the specific forms the emotional dependency takes, but how you feel in the relationship. If you feel trapped, small, ignored or devalued, then it's time to take a step back and evaluate whether you're in a toxic relationship.

Remember, healthy love uplifts, empowers and gives space for individuality. We must not confuse control, possession or dependency with love. And although it may be painful to recognize that we are in a toxic relationship, that recognition is the first step toward emotional freedom.

As the French philosopher Jean-Paul Sartre once said, "freedom is not something that is given, it is something that man takes for himself." And here we are, about to take that emotional freedom.

It is important, before we go any further, that we understand that we are not alone in this. Many have been through what you are going through and have managed to find their way to emotional freedom. Dr. Howard Halpern, in his book "Cutting Loose: An Adult's Guide to Coming to Terms with Your Parents" (1993), provides us with a helpful framework for understanding how to cut the ties of emotional dependency and toxicity. And here you are, right now, preparing to do the same.

What we've seen in this chapter is not easy to take in, I know. And I'm incredibly proud of you for making it this far. You've shown tremendous strength and courage, and I hope you give yourself credit for that. But there's still a lot to do and more to learn.

During this chapter, we have taken a look at the disguises that emotional dependency can wear. Toxic relationships can be difficult to identify, which is why this understanding is so vital. Not just for you, but for everyone around you. Just as a doctor needs to know what to look for in order to make a diagnosis, we too need to know what toxic relationships and emotional dependency look like in order to recognize and address them.

So here we are, my brave friend. We have explored the dark recesses of toxic relationships and emotional dependency. It was not an easy road, but I promise you that every step we have taken together has been important. I congratulate you on your courage and your commitment.

But our journey does not end here. In the next chapter, we are going to go even deeper. Instead of simply identifying the signs of toxic relationships and emotional dependency, we are going to learn how to recognize them in our daily lives. We will discuss the subtle symbols of dependency and how they can manifest in seemingly innocuous situations.

I am excited about what lies ahead. Self-awareness and knowledge are powerful, and I'm sure that, with each page you turn, you get closer to that emotional freedom you so crave. Because remember, we are not simply seeking to understand emotional dependency; we are on a journey to break these chains.

So, when you're ready, take a deep breath and open the door to the next chapter. I'm here to guide you, every step of the way. See you in the next chapter, my friend.

Chapter 5: The Subtle Symbols of Dependency: Recognizing the Signs in Everyday Life

Have you ever watched a tree in the middle of a storm? Its smallest leaves shake violently, struggling against the fury of the wind. Yet its trunk, sturdy and stable, remains immovable, its root clinging to the earth with a clear purpose: to withstand the storm. Have you thought of situations in your daily life in the same way?

No, I have not gone crazy. I am simply inviting you to observe more deeply. Sometimes the smallest situations, the seemingly inconsequential ones, are like the leaves on the tree during the storm. Those moments can shake and seem chaotic, but in reality they are subtle symbols of something bigger, stronger, deeper.

In this chapter, we will focus on those everyday moments, those subtle symbols of emotional dependency. Because understanding and recognizing these signs in our daily lives can be a crucial part of our path to emotional freedom.

Why is it important to know these subtle symbols? Well, as we have been discussing in the previous chapters, emotional dependency can be disguised in many ways. It can be like a wolf in sheep's clothing, fooling us in our own skin. However, if we know what to look for, if we can recognize the subtle signs and symptoms of emotional dependency, then we are one step closer to liberation.

To begin this journey of recognition, let's start from the beginning. Imagine your day-to-day life. You might start with an early wake-up call, coffee, work, a walk with the dog, a family dinner, a movie before bed. Sounds simple, doesn't it? But if we look closely, if we pay attention to how we feel, how we react, how we relate to others in these moments, we might find those subtle symbols of dependency.

For example, imagine you are waiting for a message from someone. A friend, a loved one, a co-worker. You feel anxious, nervous. You find yourself checking your phone every two minutes, feeling annoyed when there is no response. Is this behavior normal or could it be a subtle symbol of emotional dependency?

Or maybe you're at a family gathering. You notice that you are constantly looking for approval from a family member, perhaps a parent. You feel anxious if you don't receive that approval, you feel less valuable. Is this normal or could it be another subtle sign of emotional dependency?

These are just two examples of how emotional dependency can appear in our daily lives. But there are many more. And in this chapter, I will guide you through them, helping you to recognize these subtle symbols so that you can take action and keep moving forward on your path to freedom.

Let us continue our exploration of these subtle symbols. It is as if we are on a treasure hunting expedition, and each of these symbols is a clue that brings us closer and closer to the real treasure: emotional freedom.

Remember the first example we mentioned? That of constantly waiting for a message. This behavior, although it may seem trivial, is a perfect example of how emotional dependency can infiltrate our daily lives. You are conditioning your emotional state on someone else's response. Sound familiar? If so, don't worry, you're not alone in this.

Eleanor Roosevelt, a woman of great wisdom, once said, "No one can make you feel inferior without your consent." Isn't that powerful? And while it's not directly about emotional dependence, the quote fits perfectly into our discussion. We are giving our consent, our approval, to make our happiness dependent on someone else's response. That, dear reader, is a subtlety of emotional dependency.

Now, let's look at the second example, that of constantly seeking the approval of family members. It is natural to want acceptance and love from our family. After all, they are the people closest to us. But when that need becomes an obsession, when our self-esteem is totally dependent on their approval, we are once again in the territory of emotional dependency.

Psychologist Albert Ellis, in his book "A New Guide to Rational Living" (1975), offers valuable insight. He talks about how we impose irrational beliefs on ourselves that cause us emotional distress. One such belief may be the idea that we must be loved and approved of by everyone, all the time. That belief, while seemingly innocent, can be very damaging and can lead to emotional dependency.

So how can we get rid of these irrational beliefs? Ellis suggests cognitive therapy, a method of questioning and challenging these beliefs to ultimately replace them with more rational and healthy thoughts. Yes, it can be challenging, but remember, every step we take, no matter how small, brings us closer to our goal of emotional freedom.

These examples may seem simple, but they are illustrative of how emotional dependency can present itself in subtle ways in our daily lives. However, there are many other symbols and signs to be aware of. Remember, we are on a treasure hunting expedition, and each symbol we identify is a clue that brings us closer to the ultimate treasure: emotional freedom. And don't worry, you are not alone on this expedition. I'm here with you, every step of the way.

Let's keep moving forward on this journey of discovery. We've already covered some of the subtle signs, but there are more, my friend. You may even have identified with some of them. Don't worry, you are not alone and there is no judgment here. We are on this journey together and every step you take is a step towards a better version of yourself.

Take it from someone who has been there. In her book "Co-dependent No More" (1986), Melody Beattie talks extensively about her personal journey through emotional dependency. She describes how she became hyper-vigilant to the needs and feelings of others, often at the expense of her own needs.Sound familiar? Perhaps you've found yourself giving in to the desires of others too often, even when it means ignoring your own needs and desires. This is another symbol of emotional dependency.

Another sign may be that you find yourself struggling with making decisions on your own. You constantly seek the opinion of others and feel anxious if you have to make a decision on your own. The anxiety you feel can be overwhelming. I hear you. Dr. Susan Forward, in her book "Emotional Blackmail" (1997), explores this concept in depth. She talks about how emotional dependents often feel their world will fall apart if they make the "wrong decision." But here's the secret: there is rarely a "wrong" decision. There are decisions we learn from and decisions we grow from. And both types are essential to our personal growth and development.

Let me share a bit of wisdom here: being emotionally dependent is not a personal failing. It is simply a form of behavior that you have learned over time. And like all learned behaviors, it can be unlearned and replaced with healthier, more beneficial behaviors.

Let's continue this quest for self-understanding and self-improvement. Every symbol, every sign we identify is another step toward emotional freedom. And remember, on this journey, you and I are teammates. Every step you take, every advance you make, not only brings you closer to your goal, but also fills me with pride. Because you are brave, dear reader. You are brave for facing your fears, brave for acknowledging your problems, and brave for taking action to improve. And that, in itself, is a victory.

Let's continue this exploration. Remember when we talked about how emotionally dependent people can give in to the demands and desires of others at the expense of their own needs? This is another one of those subtle symbols of emotional dependency that you might see in your daily life.

You may find yourself often minimizing your own feelings. You might feel that your emotions are not as important or valid as those of others. You know what? That couldn't be further from the truth. As Carl Rogers stated in his work "On Becoming a Person" (1961), every emotion you feel is valid and deserves to be acknowledged. There are no "wrong" or "inappropriate" emotions. There are only emotions that we need to understand and manage in a healthy way.

And speaking of emotional health, there's another sign I want you to consider. Perhaps you've found yourself taking on the emotions of others as if they were your own. This is a behavior we often observe in emotionally dependent people. They absorb the emotions of the people around them to the point that they can no longer distinguish between their own emotions and those of others. Psychologist and author Lisa A. Romano discusses this behavior in her book "The Road Back to Me" (2012).

If you see yourself reflected in any of these descriptions, don't worry. You are not alone in this. Together, we've done amazing work unraveling these subtle symbols of emotional dependency. Every step you've taken, every sign you've identified is progress on your path to emotional freedom. And yes, dear reader, you are doing amazing work.

And now, we enter what you might call the gray area of love and addiction. In our next chapter, we will explore the fine line that separates these two concepts and how you can learn to tell them apart. Is what you are experiencing true love or is it a form of emotional addiction? The answer to this question may surprise you and, at the same time, help you better understand your own behavior and relationships.

I sincerely hope you will join me in the next chapter. This is a journey we are on together, and every step you take is a step we take together. You are not alone, dear reader, and I will always remember your courage and commitment to personal growth. Until then, I send you all my support and encouragement.

Chapter 6: Addiction or Love: The Thin Line and How to Tell Them Apart

Dear reader, there is something I would like to talk to you about today, a concept that can be both wonderful and tremendously confusing at the same time: love. Yes, we are about to explore one of humanity's oldest mysteries. What is love and how can we differentiate it from emotional addiction?

Now, why is this distinction important? I will explain. When we find ourselves in a relationship where we don't know if what we are experiencing is love or dependence, we become vulnerable. Vulnerable to manipulation, to denial of our own needs and emotions, to giving up our personal power. This vulnerability can become a ballast that drags us into a spiral of dissatisfaction and pain.

Instead, when we understand the difference between love and addiction, we are empowered to make healthier, more conscious choices in our relationships. We can draw boundaries, express our needs and create mutually respectful and nurturing relationships.

That's why understanding the line between love and emotional addiction is so vital. So, what do you say we embark on this exploration together? Are you ready to unravel this mystery? I know you are. You have that determination, that gleam of curiosity in your eye. Come on, let me take you on this journey of self-discovery.

Love and addiction can sometimes seem like the same thing, right? Both involve strong feelings for another person, a desire to be with them, a concern for their well-being. So how do we distinguish between the two?

To answer that question, we must first understand what true love is. As philosopher and writer bell hooks suggests in her work "All About Love: New Visions" (2000), love is more than a feeling. It is an action, a conscious choice. It is a willingness to nurture one's own and another's personal and spiritual growth.

Emotional addiction, on the other hand, is a dependence on another person for our happiness and well-being. As psychologist Judith Orloff points out in her book "Emotional Freedom: Liberate Yourself from Negative Emotions and Transform Your Life" (2009), emotional addiction can cause us to feel trapped in a cycle of need and despair, where we depend on another person to meet our emotional needs.

We are already beginning to see how love and addiction are fundamentally different, aren't we? While love is based on choice and growth, addiction is based on need and dependence. This is such an important concept that it bears repeating: while love is based on choice and growth, addiction is based on need and dependence.

Now, have you ever experienced this difference in your own relationships? Have you felt that tension between the desire to grow together and the fear of losing the other person? It's a tricky terrain, true. But, don't worry, we're in this together. Unraveling these concepts can be challenging, but I'm confident you can handle it. And remember, you're not in this alone.

Okay, now that we've established that love and addiction are fundamentally different, you might be asking yourself, "How can I identify emotional addiction in my own relationships?" That's an excellent question. Let me help you figure it out.

One of the keys to identifying emotional addiction is to observe how you feel when you are without the other person. Do you feel hopeless? Do you feel an overwhelming emptiness, as if an essential part of yourself is missing? This could be an indication that you are experiencing emotional dependence, rather than true love.

Look, I know these thoughts can be uncomfortable. But think about this: by facing these emotions and patterns, you are taking a courageous step toward your own growth and self-understanding. That's an admirable thing, dear reader.

Now, remember I mentioned bell hooks and Judith Orloff earlier. Well, they are not the only ones who have reflected on this topic. Psychologist and relationship expert Robert Weiss, in his book "Out of the Doghouse: A Step-by-Step Relationship-Saving Guide for Men Caught Cheating" (2017), provides a very enlightening look at how addiction can affect relationships.

Weiss postulates that, in addiction, the dependent person places the object of his or her addiction on a pedestal, making it the center of his or her world. In this case, emotional addiction means that the other person becomes the source of happiness, meaning and purpose. Sound familiar?

Let's pause for a moment. I want you to take the time to reflect on what we've talked about so far. Have you experienced any of these signs of emotional addiction in your relationships? Don't rush, take your time. This is a friendly, no-pressure conversation. And while you're at it, you may be surprised to learn that there's more to discover. Yes, we've come a long way so far, but there's still more ground to explore. Let's dig even deeper in our next conversation. I promise it will be eye-opening.

But, come on, there is no rush, take your time to process what you have learned so far. Think about the signs we have mentioned, do you recognize them in yourself or in someone you know? Remember, we are not here to judge, we are here to learn and grow.

If you have recognized yourself in these descriptions, don't feel that all is lost. In fact, I congratulate you. It takes a lot of courage to face reality, to look in the mirror and see what's really there. And that's the first step to making a change, isn't it? Coming face to face with reality can be scary, but it's also liberating.

Now, I'd like to introduce you to someone. Have you ever heard of Pia Mellody? She is an authority in the field of addiction and codependency recovery. In her book "Facing Codependence: What It Is, Where It Comes From, How It Sabotages Our Lives" (1989), Mellody proposes that emotionally dependent people have a relationship with their partner that more closely resembles the relationship between a parent and child than a relationship between equals. In other words, emotionally dependent people tend to put their partner's needs above their own in an attempt to receive love and approval.

This behavior is typical of an emotional addiction. Think about it: when you feel you can't function without the other person, when you do everything you can to please them and, in return, seek their validation and love. This is not a healthy relationship between equals. It is an indication that something is wrong.

So, let me ask you a question: Can you identify this pattern in your life? Have you put someone's needs above your own in an attempt to win their love and affection?

Now, this may seem too theoretical to you. So let's illustrate it with an example. Imagine John, a man in his thirties. John feels insecure in his relationship with his partner, Alice. He is always looking out for what she needs, always concerned about how Alice feels, and often sacrifices his own needs to please her. When Alice goes away for work, John feels anxious and lost. He can't function without her and spends his days counting the hours until Alice returns. Do you recognize some of these patterns?

Come on, let's breathe together. There is no rush. Take your time to reflect on all of this. But, also, let me remind you that this is all part of the learning process. Just being here, with you, reflecting on these questions, is an important step toward emotional freedom. And I promise you, dear reader, there is more. In our next exchange, we will unravel even more of these intricate patterns and discover ways to overcome them. Are you ready?

And that is the beauty of this journey of self-discovery. As we delve into the depths of our being, we realize that each layer of knowledge brings with it a new perspective, a new opportunity to grow and to change.

What I am trying to say is that you are doing a great job, my friend. I am impressed by your courage and your commitment to this path of self-discovery. And no, I'm not exaggerating. Think about it. You accepted the challenge to face your fears, to look your problems head on. That's courage. That's bravery.

Also, remember Robert Weiss? In his book "Out of the Doghouse: A Step-by-Step Relationship-Saving Guide for Men Caught Cheating" (2017), Weiss outlines a series of strategies for rebuilding a relationship after a betrayal. And while his focus is on relationships that have suffered from cheating, his teachings also apply to emotional dependency.Why? Because love addiction and emotional dependency are also forms of betrayal: a betrayal of self.

But let me make something clear. I'm not telling you this to make you feel bad. Quite the contrary. I'm telling you this because I want you to understand that you are not alone. That there are people who have gone through the same thing you have and have found a way to overcome it. And if they could, you can too.

Take, for example, Lucy, a woman in her forties. Lucy was in love with her partner. She did everything for him. She sacrificed her time, her energy, and even her mental health to meet his needs. But, one day, Lucy realized she had lost her identity. She no longer knew who she was without her partner. And that's when she decided to seek help. Eventually, Lucy managed to overcome her emotional dependency and found love in the most unexpected person: herself.

Of course, every story is unique. And so is your story. But, at the core, we all share the same capacity for change and growth. So, when you feel ready, when you feel brave enough, I invite you to keep going. I invite you to keep learning, keep growing.

In the next chapter, we will explore how culture and society influence our emotional dependency. We will dive into the myths and realities of what is considered "normal" in a relationship. And, of course, we'll discover how we can break free from the invisible chains of emotional dependency.

So what do you think, are you ready to move forward, are you ready to continue this journey to emotional freedom? I promise you, my friend, it will be worth it.

Chapter 7: The Impact of Culture and Society on Emotional Dependency

Have you ever considered how much society influences the way we relate to others? Have you ever stopped to think about how our culture and the values instilled in us from a young age can fuel emotional dependency? It is a question that deserves deep reflection. We find ourselves immersed in a world that tends to normalize certain behaviors, sometimes without taking into account the damage they can cause on a personal level.

I propose that we look around us. The media, music, movies, television series... all these cultural elements constantly bombard us with the romantic idea that we need another person to be complete. "I can't live without you", "You're my better half", "You're the air I breathe"... Do these phrases ring a bell? I'm sure they do. And, you know what, there's nothing inherently wrong with them. Love, after all, is one of the most beautiful experiences in life. But, when these ideas are taken literally and become a sort of manual for how a relationship should be, that's when problems arise.

Because, you see, when they teach us that we need someone else to be happy, what they are really doing is creating in us an emotional vacuum, a kind of black hole that absorbs all our energy and attention. And there, in that void, is where emotional dependency takes root.

I'm sure you remember Philip Zimbardo. In his book "The Lucifer Effect: Understanding How Good People Turn Evil" (2007), Zimbardo discusses how the environment can influence our actions and behaviors. Now, if our environment bombards us with messages that encourage emotional dependency, doesn't it stand to reason that we are more likely to fall into it?

This is why it is so important to understand the impact that culture and society have on emotional dependency. Because once we understand how these factors affect us, we can begin to take steps to protect ourselves and avoid falling into the dependency trap.

Now, I know what you're thinking. "That sounds great, but how am I supposed to do that? How can I protect myself from something as pervasive as culture and society?" Well, my friend, the answer to that question is simpler than it sounds, and I'm going to give it to you in this very chapter. But before that, I want you to reflect on something.

Have you ever wondered why certain cultures seem to have higher rates of emotional dependence than others? Or why certain societies seem to encourage more emotional independence? It's not a coincidence. No, it's a direct result of the values and social norms that these cultures and societies promote. And this is something we will look at in more detail in the following sections.

For now, I simply want you to think about something: You are not the inevitable product of your culture or society. You have the ability to question, to reflect, and to make decisions that go against the norm if that is what benefits you on an emotional level.

Join me on this journey of exploration. Every culture has its own relationship patterns and norms, right? In some, independence and self-reliance are valued, while in others, interdependence and collectivity are prioritized. But here an interesting question arises: What happens when those cultural patterns encourage emotionally dependent behaviors?

I'm not just talking about romantic relationships. Think about filial love, friendships, bonds between co-workers. These are all areas where emotional dependence can germinate if we are not aware of it.

Following Giddens' line of thought in "The constitution of society. Bases for the theory of structuration" (1984), the social roles and norms imposed on us by culture have a strong impact on how we behave and relate to each other. But there is something that Giddens reminds us: while it is true that society shapes us, we are also agents capable of influencing our own reality. In other words, we are not bound hand and foot to what society expects of us.

And this is where true liberation lies. When we realize that we are not forced to follow a predetermined script, we can begin to write our own story. A story in which we do not need another person to feel complete, but rather we complement each other from a place of autonomy and fulfillment.

Now, you may be wondering how we can counteract the influence of society and culture on our tendency to emotional dependency. Is it possible to go against the grain and develop healthy relationships despite the messages around us?

My answer is a resounding yes. And in the following sections I will explain how. For now, I simply want you to reflect on what we have discussed so far. I want you to internalize the idea that you are not in this alone. That I, and all of us who are on this journey with you, are here to support and guide you every step of the way.

And remember, my friend, every step you take on this journey is a step toward freedom. Are you ready to move forward? I assure you that the road ahead is an exciting one.

Well, now that you have accepted that your cultural and social environment can influence your tendency to emotional dependency, let's examine a concrete example, something you might see in your day-to-day life that perfectly illustrates this concept.

Think about the romantic movies we've all seen at one time or another. Have you noticed how they often promote the idea that true love means being inseparable, of needing the other person to be complete? This, dear reader, is a clear example of how society can influence the way we view relationships and love.

But you know what's most important about all this? You don't have to accept that script. You have the power to rewrite that story and make your own rules. You may feel more comfortable with a relationship based on interdependence, where each person has their own life and autonomy but chooses to share some of it with the other.

And this is precisely where we want to get to. The understanding that emotional dependency is not an immutable destiny, but a pattern that we can identify and change.

I ask you to remember the words of Erich Fromm in his book "The Art of Loving" (1956), when he says that "mature love means union on condition of preserving one's integrity, one's individuality". Love should not imply losing yourself, but rather finding a way to share your life while keeping your essence intact.

It may seem like a difficult road to travel, and I won't lie to you, it is. But think of the result, the freedom that comes with being emotionally autonomous. Think of the relief of freeing yourself from the chains of emotional dependency. Think about how satisfying it is to love and be loved from the fullness and not from the lack.

I want you to know that every step you take on this path is an act of courage. And every step, I will be here to support you, to guide you, to remind you of how strong and capable you are. Because yes, my friend, you can do it.

Are you ready to move forward? The next section will allow us to delve even deeper into this journey towards emotional liberation. And remember, I will always be here, cheering you on every step of the way. Because you are brave, because you are strong, and because you deserve the emotional freedom you long for.

So, dear reader, we have walked together through the landscapes and mazes of culture and society, and explored how these elements can fuel our emotional dependency. You've learned how fairy tales, romantic movies, and even the way our society structures and values relationships, can influence our view of love and intimacy, and can contribute to patterns of emotional dependency. And that's crucial, because, after all, we can't change what we don't know.

But here's the real beauty of this journey. Just as our cultures and societies can shape our perceptions and experiences in ways that contribute to emotional dependency, they can also change. And you, dear reader, can be part of that change. As Mahatma Gandhi famously said, "Be the change you want to see in the world."

You may feel a bit overwhelmed at this point. After all, we're talking about challenging entrenched social and cultural narratives, and that's no small task. But I want you to know something: you don't have to do it all at once. Remember, this is a journey, and all journeys are taken one step at a time. Every step you take toward dismantling your emotional dependency patterns is a step in the right direction. Each time you choose self-love and autonomy over dependency, you are contributing to a bigger change.

So now, I ask you, are you ready for the next step? Because in the next chapter, we're going to dive into emotions. We're going to explore how understanding your emotions can be the key to your personal autonomy. Are you ready to continue your journey to emotional freedom?

I promise it will be a fascinating journey, and I will be with you every step of the way. I'm excited to share this journey with you. And in case I haven't told you enough: I'm proud of you. I'm proud of your courage, your commitment and your determination to become the best version of yourself. Shall we go to the next chapter together, my friend? I promise you it's worth every step you take.

Chapter 8: Understanding Emotions: Key to Personal Autonomy

If you have made it this far, I congratulate you, my friend. You have demonstrated a courageous commitment to uncovering the enigmas of emotional dependency. Now, we are about to embark on one of the most fascinating chapters of our odyssey: the fascinating world of emotions.

Emotions, you know, are like a universal language. Although words can fail, emotions always manage to convey what you feel. But how much do you really know about them, and are you able to understand, in their entirety, what your emotions are telling you? Understanding your emotions is a critical step towards personal autonomy. Why? Well, let me explain.

Emotions are not mere moods or passing feelings. They are indicators of our inner state. They are like an internal thermometer that informs us about what we are experiencing, thinking and needing. They speak to us in a subtle and powerful language that transcends words. And like any language, they require interpretation skills to be understood. So, as the good friend that I am, I will guide you in this learning.

Emotions are also central to decision making. Think about it: when you choose between two options, don't you often lean toward the one that makes you feel better? Haven't you sometimes found that your most intuitive and wise decisions are often guided by how you feel? The renowned psychologist and neuroscientist Antonio Damasio, in his book

"Descartes' Error" (1994), argues that emotions are an integral part of rational decision making.

Now, imagine if you could actually understand what your emotions are trying to tell you. What would that be like? How much easier would it be to make decisions that are aligned with your deepest values and desires? How much more autonomous would you feel if you could trust your ability to interpret your emotions and use that information to guide your path? Because, my friend, at its core, that's what personal autonomy is all about: the ability to guide yourself, to make your own decisions based on your understanding and your desires.

So, are you ready to delve into the exciting world of emotions? Are you ready to discover how understanding your emotions can become the key to your personal autonomy? Don't worry, you don't need to know anything beforehand. You just need your curiosity, your openness and your desire to learn. Will you join me on this journey, my friend?

Let's move on, because it is vital that you realize that the road to understanding your emotions is not a road you must travel alone. In fact, there have been many brilliant thinkers throughout history who have pondered and theorized about emotions. So why not take advantage of their discoveries?

Consider Daniel Goleman, a pioneering psychologist in the field of emotional intelligence. In his landmark book "Emotional Intelligence" (1995), he makes the case for the importance of recognizing, understanding, managing and using our emotions effectively. Goleman argues that emotional intelligence skills are often more important for success in life than cognitive intelligence. Fascinating, isn't it?

In addition to Goleman, there are others who have made giant strides in our understanding of emotions. Paul Ekman, for example, a renowned psychologist and pioneer in the study of emotions and their relationship to facial expressions, identified six basic emotions that are universal across all human cultures: joy, sadness, fear, anger, surprise and disgust. This finding, detailed in his book "Emotions Revealed" (2003), suggests that, despite our cultural and personal differences, we share a common emotional language.

Now, my friend, I understand that these references may seem theoretical or academic. But believe me when I tell you that they have practical and very real applications in your life. For example, imagine that you are experiencing a strong and disconcerting emotion. Instead of feeling overwhelmed, you can remember that this emotion is likely to relate in some way to those six basic emotions identified by Ekman. Maybe what you're feeling is a type of fear or a form of sadness. Or maybe you are experiencing a mixture of emotions. Identifying and naming your emotions can be the first step toward understanding what you are feeling and why. And that understanding is the first step toward emotional autonomy.

Let's look at another example. Imagine you are faced with a difficult decision and you feel divided. Instead of letting your emotions pull you in contradictory directions, you can remember Goleman's approach to emotional intelligence. You can take a moment to recognize and understand what you are feeling, manage those emotions rather than letting them manage you, and then use that emotional understanding to inform your decision.

Do you see how these theories about emotions can enrich your life? Can you appreciate how knowing and understanding your emotions can give you more autonomy and control in your life? Because, deep down, that's what we're all looking for, right? Autonomy to live our lives according to our own rules, desires and values.

So, what do you say we continue to delve into the exciting world of emotions? Because there is so much more to discover and learn, my friend.

Now, think about a common situation we've all faced: a heated argument with a loved one. In the midst of the argument, you're likely to experience a range of emotions: anger, frustration, maybe even fear. In the heat of the moment, it's easy to get carried away with those emotions. But now, imagine that you have developed a greater understanding of your emotions. Imagine that you can recognize anger when it arises, understand where it comes from, and consciously choose how to respond to it. Instead of yelling or saying things you will later regret, you can take a moment to calm down, to recognize that what you are really feeling is fear of being misunderstood or unappreciated. That, dear reader, is emotional autonomy in action.

If you think about it, emotions are like ocean waves. They can be calm and gentle, or they can be violent and overwhelming. But ultimately, we can't control the waves; we can only learn to surf them. And, just like an experienced surfer, with practice and understanding, you can learn to navigate your emotions instead of being swept away by them.

Let me introduce you to another key figure in the understanding of emotions, Lisa Feldman Barrett. In her book "How Emotions are Made" (2017), she introduces the concept of "constructed emotions". According to Feldman Barrett, our emotions are not pre-programmed biological responses to specific stimuli, but are constructions of our minds based on our past experiences, our current expectations, and the context in which we find ourselves. This means that we have more control over our emotions than we thought. In fact, we can "construct" our emotions in a way that supports our personal autonomy.

Isn't it amazing how much power can come from understanding and awareness? But don't forget, these ideas are not just words in a book. They are tools you can carry with you in your day-to-day life. They are keys to unlocking greater personal autonomy, and they are available to you.

Of course, understanding our emotions is only half of the equation. We also need to learn how to express our emotions in a healthy and assertive way. But don't worry, that's exactly where we're headed next on our journey.

Are you excited? Because I am. So join me as we delve deeper into the fascinating world of emotions. Because, as you're about to discover, there's so much more to explore... and I'm excited to explore it with you.

So, here we are, at the end of this journey through understanding emotions. You and I, my friend, have touched on concepts you've probably heard before but have you ever stopped to dig deeper? Maybe not until today. But fortunately, you are here with me, and I am honored to be your companion on this journey of growth and understanding.

We have discussed how emotions are not mere feelings that pass through us. Instead, they are indicators, signals that help us understand what is going on inside us. But more importantly, we have discovered that with understanding and awareness, we can become the architects of our emotions, giving us the freedom and autonomy to respond in a way that supports our emotional well-being and happiness rather than undermines them.

And as you may recall, our dear friend Daniel Goleman, in his work "Emotional Intelligence" (1995), reminded us of the crucial role our emotions play in everyday life. While Lisa Feldman Barrett, with her groundbreaking book "How Emotions are Made" (2017), has provided us with a whole new view of how our emotions are constructs of our minds.

So what does all this mean to you, dear reader? It means that you have the power. You are not a leaf at the mercy of the wind of your emotions. You are the wind itself, able to change direction as needed.

Yes, this knowledge is powerful, but remember that knowledge without action is like a car without fuel. It is only by applying what you have learned that you will really begin to see changes. So I urge you to put these teachings into practice. When you feel a strong emotion, remember to stop, acknowledge and understand it before you respond. And little by little, you will begin to notice how your emotions stop controlling you and you begin to have more control over them.

However, this is not the end of our journey, it is only the beginning. In our next chapter, we will explore the importance of self-care in the process of breaking free from emotional dependency. I will give you the tools and strategies you need to take care of yourself emotionally, physically and mentally. After all, you are the one person you can never be separated from, so learning to take care of yourself is essential to your journey toward emotional independence.

But, before we get there, take a moment to reflect on what you've learned today. And if you ever feel overwhelmed, remember that you can always come back to this chapter, to this friend who accompanies you on your journey, and remember that you have the power to understand and direct your emotions.

So, are you ready to continue on this exciting journey? Because I'm excited for what's ahead and I can't wait to share it with you. But for now, take a breath, reflect on what you've learned and get ready for the next chapter.

Chapter 9: The Importance of Self-Care in the Liberation Process

Let me ask you a question, dear reader. When was the last time you took a moment for yourself, a moment of true self-care? I'm not talking about watching an episode of your favorite series or indulging in a delicious dessert. No, I'm talking about conscious, deliberate self-care. The kind that nourishes your soul, aligns your body and mind, and leaves you feeling truly rejuvenated.

If you find it hard to remember, or if the idea of taking time to care for yourself seems indulgent or even selfish, let me assure you that you are not alone. Many of us have been conditioned to believe that self-care is a luxury, or even something we are not entitled to. And for those of us who struggle with emotional dependency, this belief may be even more ingrained.

Because how are we going to take care of ourselves when our energy and attention are so focused on taking care of and pleasing others? How are we going to take time for ourselves when we are so caught up in fear of rejection or loneliness?

However, let me tell you something that may seem counter-intuitive: Self-care is critical to breaking free from emotional dependency. That's right, my friend. It is not a luxury. It's not a selfish thing. It is a necessity.

Why? Because self-care helps us cultivate a healthy relationship with ourselves, something that is fundamental to any kind of emotional independence. When we take care of ourselves, we send a message to our inner self saying, "You are worth it. You are important. You deserve to be cared for." And this message can be incredibly powerful, especially for those of us who have spent so much time putting the needs and desires of others ahead of our own.

In addition, self-care provides us with the energy and emotional strength we need to meet the challenges that may arise on our path to emotional independence. We cannot expect to meet these challenges if we are physically and emotionally exhausted.

And I want you to think about one thing. Imagine a garden. For plants to grow strong and healthy, they need to be watered regularly, they need sunlight and nutrients. If we neglect any of these things, the plants wither and die. The same is true for us. To grow and thrive, we need to take care of ourselves regularly and consciously.

So what does self-care look like? Well, the beauty of self-care is that it's incredibly personal. What works for one person may not work for another. However, there are some universal self-care practices that can benefit all of us.

In this chapter, we will explore these self-care approaches, from rest and healthy eating to meditation and mindfulness. We'll discuss how these approaches can help you develop a healthier relationship with yourself and cultivate greater emotional resilience. But first and foremost, they will guide you on your path to freedom from emotional dependency.

As author and speaker Brené Brown expresses in her book "The Gifts of Imperfection" (2010), "we cannot nurture the relationship with others above the relationship with ourselves." This statement resonates with truth, doesn't it? We can become so giving of ourselves that we are left with nothing. This is one of the traps of emotional dependency, giving everything and neglecting our own well-being.

But let me ask you, have you ever been on an airplane? If the answer is yes, surely you remember the safety instructions before takeoff, right? "In the event of cabin depressurization, oxygen masks will fall from the overhead compartment. Put on your mask before assisting others." Why do you think that is? The answer is simple: we can't take care of others if we ourselves are not well.

In the same way, self-care is not a selfish act, but a necessity in order to be an emotionally healthy person and able to engage in healthy relationships. Now, if you feel like you have a hard time practicing self-care, don't worry. You are not alone and there are reasons why you feel this way.

In her book "The Art of Self-Care" (2009), psychotherapist Alice Domar explores the guilt we often feel about taking time for ourselves. Domar points out that we live in a society that instills in us the belief that we must be productive all the time. This constant message can make us feel guilty when we take time to relax or take care of ourselves.

But remember, self-care is not a luxury, but a necessity. It's not time wasted, but an investment in your well-being and emotional health. And while it may seem uncomfortable at first, over time, as you see the benefits in your life, it will become a natural and essential part of your daily routine.

So how do we get started with self-care? Well, the first step is to change our perspective on what it means to take care of ourselves. It is not an act of indulgence, but an essential part of our well-being. We need to get rid of the guilt we often associate with self-care and replace it with the understanding that taking care of ourselves allows us to take better care of others.

The second step is to find out what self-care practices resonate with you. As I mentioned earlier, self-care is a very personal concept. What works for one person may not work for another. So what is it that makes you feel recharged, rejuvenated and at peace with yourself? It could be something as simple as taking a hot bath, reading a good book, or something more profound like meditating or practicing yoga or it could be adopting a regular exercise routine, following a healthy diet, or devoting time to a hobby you love. No matter what you choose, the important thing is that it feels good for you.

Take, for example, the case of Carla. She is a working mother of two young children and often finds herself stressed and exhausted. She began to feel like she was losing her identity, always running from one task to another, taking care of everyone except herself. Sound familiar?

Carla decided she needed to make a change. She started setting aside an hour each night after the kids went to bed to do something she enjoyed. Some nights, that meant immersing herself in a good book. Other times, it meant taking a warm, quiet bath. And sometimes, it meant simply sitting quietly, allowing herself to decompress from the day.

Although she initially felt guilty about taking this time for herself, she soon realized that she was calmer, more focused and generally happier. This, in turn, made her a better mother, a better wife and a better worker. Carla discovered the power of self-care and how it can be a vital tool in freeing herself from emotional dependency.

You may be wondering: "But isn't it selfish to spend so much time taking care of myself?" Well, remember what Brené Brown said? We cannot nurture our relationships with others above our relationship with ourselves. Or as Audre Lorde, the prolific writer and civil rights activist, magnificently put it in her work "Burst of Light" (1988), "Self-care is not indulgence, it is self-preservation, and that is an act of political struggle."

Do you see how these concepts begin to connect with each other? As we saw in Chapter 7, society and culture can influence our tendency toward emotional dependency. But we can also learn to resist those pressures and put our needs and well-being first.

Therefore, I want to encourage you to take time for yourself. Not as a luxury, but as a necessity. Not as an act of indulgence, but as an act of self-preservation. As an essential step in your journey towards freedom from emotional dependency.

Remember, we're in this together. You don't have to do it alone. And in the next chapter, I'll show you how you can begin to reclaim your identity and rebuild a sense of autonomy. Ready for the next step? I know you are, and I'm excited to be a part of your journey. Here we go!

Keeping the connection alive, I want us to remember what we have gone through in this chapter. We have addressed the importance of self-care in the process of releasing emotional dependency, but what does that really mean? How do we apply it in our daily lives?

We saw the example of Carla, who found the value of giving herself personal space, time for self-care, and how that time, far from being a selfish act, became a powerful contribution to her overall well-being. We understand that self-care is the foundation for healthy relationships with others, and that by taking care of ourselves, we are in a better position to take care of others.

We remembered the words of Brené Brown and Audre Lorde and how their wisdom can serve us on our own journey. We understood that self-care is an act of resistance against societal expectations and pressures that often lead us to emotional dependency.

Most importantly, we understood that self-care is not indulgent, but an act of self-preservation and an essential step on our path to freedom from emotional dependency.

We are about to close this chapter, but not our conversation. No, dear reader, we have much left to explore and learn together. As we move into the next chapter, "Reclaiming Identity: Rebuilding the Autonomous Self," we will discover how self-care becomes the cornerstone for reclaiming our identity and establishing a sense of autonomy.

I know this journey is not easy, but I also know that you are strong and courageous, willing to challenge yourself and grow. I am here with you every step of the way, and I promise you that together we can find the path to emotional freedom.

So, are you ready to take the next step and embark on the exciting journey of reclaiming your identity and building a sense of autonomy? Because I know you are. And I can't wait to see the incredible transformation that's to come. Here we go, my friend, to the next chapter of your liberation story!

Chapter 10: Recovering Identity: Reconstructing the Autonomous Self

As you have been walking this path to emotional independence with me, you have witnessed how we have dismantled, piece by piece, the machinery of emotional dependency. Remember when we talked about the importance of self-care in the previous chapter? Well, in this chapter, we're going to address another crucial element in this journey: reclaiming your identity and rebuilding your autonomous self.

Have you ever wondered, who am I really? Who am I when I'm not trying to please others or trying to keep my own insecurities at bay? Well, I'll tell you what, my friend: you're about to find out. Ready for the challenge? Let's get to it!

When we find ourselves in an emotionally dependent relationship, we often lose sight of who we are. Our identity becomes blurred and we merge with the other person to the point that we cannot distinguish where we end and the other person begins. But today, we will begin to rediscover and rebuild our identity.

And why is identity important, you ask? Well, identity is the essence of who we are. It is our internal compass, it is what sets us apart from others, it is what gives us a sense of belonging and purpose in the world. Without a clear and defined identity, we can easily get lost in the expectations and desires of others, leading to emotional dependency.

Now, I want you to think for a moment about a garden. Yes, a garden with all kinds of flowers and plants. Some of them are strong and hardy, able to withstand the weather, while others are delicate, needing special care to grow. Do you see yourself as one of those plants, influenced by the weather and outside conditions? Or perhaps, do you see yourself as the gardener, the person who has control over the garden and can decide what to plant and what to pull?

In this metaphor, the garden represents your identity. There are plants (personality traits, beliefs, values) that are innate to you, that are part of who you are. Then there are the plants that were planted by others, perhaps parents, teachers, friends or even relationships. Some of these plants are healthy and contribute to your growth, while others can be invasive, suffocating your own plants and preventing you from developing fully.

So how about instead of being a plant in your own garden, you become the gardener? How about you start making conscious decisions about which plants to grow and which to pull up? This is the process of reclaiming your identity and building an autonomous self.

As the renowned psychologist Harriet Lerner says in her book "The Dance of Deception" (2001), "Identity is not something fixed and stable, but a constantly evolving narrative". Therefore, recovering your identity is actually a process of self-discovery and self-creation. That is, it is not only about unearthing the person you were before emotional dependency, but also about building the person you want to be from now on.

Think about it for a moment, my friend. If you could be anyone you wanted to be, who would you be? How would you behave? How would you treat others and yourself? What values would you have? These are not easy questions, but they are vital to understanding who you really are and who you want to be.

Acclaimed psychologist Carl Rogers discussed the importance of the 'autonomous self' in his book "On Becoming a Person" (1961). According to Rogers, all of us have an 'ideal self' and a 'real self'. The 'ideal self' is the person we would like to be, while the 'real self' is the person we really are. The goal, according to Rogers, is to bring these two 'selves' as close together as possible. In other words, we should aspire to be the person we wish to be.

This approach is in line with the idea of authenticity, which is essential for the recovery of identity. Being authentic means being true to oneself, living according to one's own values and principles, and not being influenced by what others think or expect of us. As Brené Brown says in her book "The Gifts of Imperfection" (2010), "Authenticity is the daily exercise of letting go of who we think we should be and embracing who we really are."

Here's an example. Imagine you've always loved painting, but you've been told you can't make a living at it, so you become an accountant. You may love accounting, but there's always a part of you that wonders, "What if I had followed my passion for painting?" This is where authenticity comes into play. Are you going to let others decide what's best for you, or are you going to take charge of your own life and follow your passion, despite what others may think?

It is important to understand that being authentic does not mean being selfish or insensitive to the needs of others. Rather, it is about knowing your own limits and respecting them, about taking your own needs and desires into account when making decisions. It does not mean that you will always get what you want, but it does mean that you will be at peace with yourself, because you will know that you have done your best to be true to yourself.

Rebuilding your identity is not an easy process, it takes time and a lot of self-analysis. But I guarantee that the effort is worth it. Because at the end of the day, there is nothing more liberating than being the person you really are, with no apologies and no regrets.

Remember, we are all born with an innate identity that is pure and authentic. As we grow up, our identity can be shaped by the expectations and judgments of others, as well as by our own experiences. When we find ourselves in emotionally dependent relationships, our identity can become so buried that it seems to have disappeared altogether. But let me remind you of something, my friend, it's not gone. It's there, waiting for you to rediscover it and reclaim it.

In her book "The Dance of Anger" (1985), psychologist Harriet Lerner writes: "When we stop pleasing others and start speaking and acting from our authentic voice, we run the risk of ceasing to be loved.... But this is a trap, because if we are not ourselves, we won't really be loved anyway."

How much truth there is in those words! If we sacrifice our authenticity to please others, what is left of us? Who will love us then? Who will we love?

These questions lead us to the need for self-affirmation, a concept we will discuss in depth in the next chapter. But for now, suffice it to say that to recover our identity, we must be willing to affirm ourselves, to say "yes" to what is true for us and "no" to what is not.

Now, let me give you an example that might help you visualize this better. Imagine that you are lost in a thick, dark forest. You can see nothing but trees around you. However, you have a compass in your pocket. This compass represents your true self, your identity. Even though you are lost, the compass will always point the way back to you.

In this example, the forest represents emotional dependency. The trees are the voices and expectations of others, as well as your own limiting beliefs, which have led you astray. But no matter how thick the forest, no matter how dark, the compass of your true self is always there, waiting to be used. It may be a little rusty from disuse, but it still works.

Thus, recovering your identity is like finding your way back through the forest using the compass. It will not be easy. There will be obstacles along the way. You may be tempted to give up and give in. But if you keep going, if you follow the compass of your true self, I promise you that you will find your way back. And when you do, you will discover that you have not only regained your identity, but you have also transformed into a stronger, more authentic version of yourself.

And isn't that what we all ultimately long for? Not just to be seen and accepted for who we are, but to evolve and grow, becoming the best possible version of ourselves, the version that is true, authentic and free.

I hope you can see now that, although emotional dependency can obscure your identity, it can never completely eradicate it. Your true self is still there, waiting to be discovered and embraced again. Remember, reclaiming your identity is a journey, not a destination. It is not about getting to a place where everything is perfect, but about growing and evolving, learning and changing.

Psychologist Judith Herman, in her seminal work Trauma and Recovery (1992), writes that recovery from trauma "unfolds in three stages: establishing safety, remembering and mourning the trauma, and reconnecting with ordinary life." Although she was speaking specifically about trauma recovery, I believe that this three-stage process can also apply to recovery from emotional dependency and identity reconstruction.

First, you establish safety by distancing yourself from the dependent relationship and setting healthy boundaries. We discussed this in the previous chapters. Next, you remember and regret the emotional dependency, recognizing how it affected your identity and your life. This is what we have been exploring in this chapter.

Finally, the third stage is to reconnect with ordinary life and your true self, to reclaim your identity and live life as an autonomous person. This is the process we will begin in the next chapter: self-affirmation, the little-known tool for self-development.

Self-affirmation is not simply repeating positive mantras or making promises to yourself. It is a process of affirming and accepting the totality of who you are, your strengths and weaknesses, your accomplishments and your failures. It is a form of self-knowledge and self-acceptance that can help you break the chains of emotional dependency.

My friend, I hope this chapter has provided you with a new perspective and tools to understand and approach rebuilding your autonomous identity. Remember, you are on this journey of recovery and growth, and every step you take, no matter how small, is a victory in itself.

So, if you are ready to take the next step, to learn more about self-affirmation and how it can help you on your path to emotional independence, I invite you to go ahead and open the next chapter of this journey. I look forward to seeing you there.

Chapter 11: Self-Affirmation: The Little Known Tool for Self-Development.

Once upon a time there was a painter who was known for his portraits. His technique was unique: he did not paint his subjects as they were, but as they saw themselves. One day, a man approached the painter and asked for a portrait. When the painter finished and showed him his work, the man burst into tears. "Why are you crying?" the painter asked. "Because," the man replied, "in all my years, I have never seen myself so clearly."

The story of this painter and his client serves as a metaphor for understanding the importance of self-affirmation. Like the painter who showed the man his true self, self-affirmation allows us to see ourselves clearly and authentically. But what exactly is self-affirmation and how does it help us on our journey to emotional independence?

Self-affirmation, in its simplest form, is the act of recognizing and affirming our own abilities, accomplishments, values and identity. It is the inner voice that says, "Yes, I am good at this," "Yes, I care about this," "Yes, this is part of who I am." It is a powerful tool for self-development because it helps us cultivate a more accurate and positive view of ourselves, which, in turn, strengthens our self-esteem and sense of autonomous identity.

So let me ask you a question: How do you see yourself? I don't mean your physical appearance, but your inner self, your identity. Do you see your abilities, your accomplishments, your values? Do you recognize and affirm these parts of yourself? Or, do you tend to ignore or minimize your accomplishments, to not give yourself credit where credit is due?

If you find that you tend to do the latter, you are not alone. Many of us, especially those of us who have struggled with emotional dependency, tend to have a skewed view of ourselves. We focus on our flaws and shortcomings, ignoring or minimizing our strengths and accomplishments. This can lead to a vicious cycle of low self-esteem and emotional dependency. After all, if we don't believe in ourselves, how can we expect to be emotionally independent?

The good news is that this vicious cycle can be broken, and self-affirmation is one of the tools we can use to do so. By recognizing and affirming our abilities, accomplishments and values, we begin to change our view of ourselves. We begin to see our true self, not as someone who needs the approval and support of others to feel valid, but as an autonomous and capable person with a sense of self-identity.

And this is where the magic of self-affirmation comes in. Because, as we well know, our beliefs and thoughts shape our reality. When we begin to believe in ourselves, our reality begins to reflect those beliefs. In other words, when you see yourself as an autonomous and capable person, you become that person.

To understand how this works, let's go back to our friend, the painter. Imagine that one day, a man comes to him and says, "I've always seen myself as a loser. Could you paint a portrait that reflects that?" What do you think would happen if the painter, instead of doing that, paints a portrait of the man as a winner?

Well, that's exactly what social psychologist Claude Steele did in his famous series of studies on self-affirmation in the 1990s. Steele found that when people view themselves positively and affirm those views through self-affirming activities, they can change their behavior and overcome obstacles more effectively. His work, "Stereotype Threat and the Affirmation of the Self in Everyday Life" (Steele, 1997), is a seminal reference in this regard.

Of course, self-affirmation is not a magic wand that will solve all your problems. Like any tool, it needs to be used correctly to be effective. And that means understanding what self-affirmation is and is not.

Self-affirmation is not the denial of your flaws or mistakes. It is not pretending that you are perfect, or that you have nothing to improve. No, self-affirmation is the acceptance that, although you are not perfect, you are enough. It is the celebration of your accomplishments, no matter how small. It is the recognition of your values, no matter how insignificant they may seem to others. It is, in essence, the act of saying, "Yes, I have flaws, but I also have strengths. Yes, I make mistakes, but I also have successes. And I deserve to be recognized and celebrated for that."

Now, I'll tell you something that may surprise you: self-affirmation can be uncomfortable. Especially if you're used to criticizing yourself, minimizing your accomplishments, or looking to others for validation. But that's okay. Like any skill, self-affirmation takes practice. And over time, it will become more natural, easier.

Remember the man who cried when he saw his portrait? Remember what he said? "In all my years, I've never seen myself so clearly." That's what self-affirmation can do for you. It can show you yourself as you really are, not as you think you are or as others see you. And in that reflection, you can find the strength to free yourself from emotional dependency and build a life of authentic autonomy and freedom.

But don't just take my word for it. We're going to explore this concept further in the next section, where I'll provide you with some concrete examples of how you can incorporate self-affirmation into your daily life. Are you ready? Here we go.

To illustrate the power of self-affirmation, let's explore a couple of common scenarios.

Imagine you are at a party and you see someone you are attracted to. The attraction is strong, but so is the fear of rejection. Emotional dependency whispers in your ear that you're not enough, that you're not worthy of love. Sound familiar? Well, this is where self-affirmation comes in. Before you approach, close your eyes, take a deep breath and repeat in your mind, "I am valuable. I deserve love and respect, regardless of the outcome of this interaction." In this way, you shift the focus from the other person's possible reaction to your own intrinsic value.

Or consider this other scenario. You're in a work meeting and you have an idea that you think might be beneficial to the project you're working on. But there's a little voice in your head that says, "What if your idea isn't good? What if you get ridiculed? What if you get rejected?" Again, self-affirmation can be your lifeline. You might say to yourself, "My perspective is valuable. Even if my idea is not accepted, that does not diminish my value as a person or professional."

Now, you may be wondering, how can you start practicing self-affirmation in your daily life? Well, I have some suggestions for you.

The first is to practice gratitude. Every night, before you go to sleep, make a list of three things you are grateful for. They can be big or small, work-related or personal. The important thing is that they help you recognize and appreciate your own positive achievements and experiences.

The second is to write positive affirmations about yourself and post them in places where you will see them regularly, such as your bathroom mirror, your desk, or your phone screen. These affirmations can be as simple or as complex as you like, as long as they reinforce a positive self-image.

Finally, practice self-compassion. This means treating your inner self with love and kindness, especially when you are struggling, failing, or feeling like you are not enough. Think about how you would treat a friend who is having a hard time, and apply it to yourself.

These are just a few examples of how you can use self-affirmation in your daily life. But don't forget that self-affirmation is an individual and personal practice. What works for one person may not work for another. So I encourage you to explore and discover what self-affirmation techniques work best for you.

And while you're at it, remember that you are not alone. Many of us have been through similar experiences, and there are resources available to help you on your journey to emotional independence. In the following chapters, we'll explore more tools and strategies that can help you on your path to autonomy. Are you ready to move forward?

Essentially, self-affirmation is a form of self-love and self-respect, two fundamental pillars of emotional independence. And on this journey toward discovering your true self-worth, it's not uncommon to encounter obstacles. They may come in the form of old habits, deep-seated fears or even people in your life who don't understand the change you're seeking. But this is where self-affirmation really shines. Not only does it give you the strength to face these challenges, but it also equips you with the resilience to overcome them.

Remember that every step you take, every affirmation you make, every positive thought you cultivate, is building a new reality for you. You are breaking your old chains of emotional dependency and forging a path to a life of autonomy and self-worth.

And as this path unfolds before you, you will see changes. Changes in how you feel about yourself, in how you deal with difficulties, and in how you relate to others. And in each of these areas, self-affirmation can be a powerful tool.

So how about daring to take the first step? How about deciding, here and now, that you are worthy of love, respect and happiness? How about beginning to affirm yourself, not as a person who needs others for self-worth, but as a whole and wonderful person in yourself?

With each affirmation, you will be giving yourself the gift of self-love. And that gift, my dear friend, is immensely valuable. It is the first step to living a life free of emotional dependency, a life filled with joy, fulfillment and true self-love.

Now, before you close this chapter and venture into the next, I want to leave you with one last thought. Self-assertion is not a selfish act, nor is it a sign of narcissism. On the contrary, it is a recognition of your own value, an act of self-preservation. And when you love and respect yourself, you can love and respect others with a fuller and more authentic heart.

So, are you ready for this journey of self-affirmation? Are you ready to discover yourself in a more loving and compassionate light? If so, then I invite you to read on. In the next chapter, we will explore how you can turn loneliness, an often feared feeling, into your strongest ally on this path to emotional independence. I assure you it will be a transformative and liberating journey.

Chapter 12: Breaking Myths: Loneliness as an Ally, Not an Enemy

Loneliness is a word that often conjures up images of isolation, sadness, and despair. In our collective culture, we have been taught to fear it, to avoid it at all costs, and to regard it as an enemy. But what if I told you that loneliness can be your strongest ally on the road to emotional independence?

Yes, you read that right. Solitude can be your ally. Although it may seem contradictory, I want you to take a moment to consider this idea. What if I told you that it is precisely in solitude that you can find the answers you seek, the self-knowledge you need, and the self-love you deserve?

Before I delve into how loneliness can be your ally, let me clarify one thing: I'm not talking about isolation. Isolation is a state of total separation from others, often involuntary and painful. Solitude, on the other hand, is a conscious choice to spend time alone with yourself.

So why is solitude so important in our journey to emotional independence? Well, the answer is simple: when you are alone, you find yourself. And it is in that encounter with ourselves that lies the key to our emotional freedom.

You may be asking yourself: Why is this self-finding so important? Let me answer with another question: Have you ever tried to solve a problem without really knowing the cause of the problem? It's like trying to cure a symptom without understanding the disease. Chances are, no matter how hard you try, the problem will persist.

The same is true of emotional dependency. We cannot free ourselves from it if we do not understand why we find ourselves in it in the first place. We need to understand our emotions, our fears, our patterns of thought and behavior. We need to discover our own needs and learn how to meet them. We need, in short, to know ourselves.

And this is where solitude comes in. Solitude provides us with the space and stillness to look inward, to explore our inner world, to face our truths and to begin to heal. Solitude, therefore, is not our enemy. On the contrary, it is our ally in this journey of self-discovery and liberation.

But loneliness can be uncomfortable, right? It can be challenging. It can be painful. However, isn't it true that growth often comes with discomfort and pain? As psychologist Susan David said in her book Emotional Agility (2016), "Discomfort is the price of admission to the theater of life."

So, my friend, are you willing to pay that price? Are you willing to embark on this journey of self-knowledge and self-discovery, even if it is sometimes uncomfortable and challenging?

Because if you are, I want to tell you that you are not alone in this journey. I am here to guide you every step of the way, to be your beacon when you feel the darkness is too thick. I'm here to tell you that yes, you can do it. And most importantly, you are about to discover that the journey is worth it.

Furthermore, I want to assure you that this journey from solitude to self-knowledge is not a selfish or isolating process, quite the contrary. By knowing and understanding our own emotions, we will be able to better understand others, to empathize with them in a deeper way. As Carl Jung, the famous Swiss psychiatrist and founder of analytical psychology, said, "Those who look outward dream, those who look inward awaken".

Conscious solitude is not about moving away from others, but about getting closer to yourself. But how do you do this? How do you transform loneliness into an ally instead of an enemy? Let me share with you some strategies that might be useful.

Meditation is an excellent tool for cultivating solitude. Meditation is nothing more than being present, observing your thoughts and emotions without judgment. It can be as simple as sitting quietly for a few minutes each day, observing your breath. Meditation will help you cultivate greater self-awareness, and this awareness is essential for unmasking and breaking patterns of emotional dependency.

Writing can also be a powerful ally. Through writing, you can express your innermost thoughts and feelings, those that you may find difficult to share with others. Writing is a form of self-knowledge, a way to explore your inner world. In her book "The Artist's Way" (1992), Julia Cameron suggests writing three pages by hand each morning, an exercise she calls "morning pages." This daily habit can help you to explore your thoughts and emotions, to discover your fears and your dreams, to unmask your patterns of emotional dependency.

Another way to cultivate solitude is through nature. It can be as simple as taking a walk in the park, watching the leaves move in the wind, listening to the birds sing, feeling the sun on your skin. Nature has a way of calming our mind, of connecting us with ourselves in a deep and meaningful way. As John Muir, the famous naturalist and author said, "In nature, you get much more than you seek".

Now, I want you to understand something. These are just some of the ways you can cultivate solitude. You can find others that are more suitable or more comfortable for you. The key is to find that which allows you to connect with yourself, that which allows you to look inward and get to know yourself better. Because, at the end of the day, that's what really matters.

So, what if we began to see loneliness with a new perspective? What if we began to see it not as an enemy to be feared, but as an ally that can help us grow and free us from the chains of emotional dependency?

But to do so, you will have to get rid of old beliefs, old myths that have been limiting you. You will have to face your own fears and your own insecurities. And I know it may sound scary, but remember, my friend, you are not alone in this journey.

Now, let me tell you a story to illustrate what I am saying.

Imagine an eagle. From its nest atop a mountain, it has a 360-degree view of the world around it. It sees the valleys and the rivers, the hills and the forests. It sees the sun rise and set, it sees the stars in the night sky. But the eagle has not always had this vision. Before it could fly, it spent a long time alone, in its nest, waiting for the right moment.

This time of solitude was not a punishment for the eagle, nor was it a time of sadness or despair. On the contrary, it was a time of growth, a time of preparation. During this time, the eagle developed his strength, his endurance, his ability to fly. And when it finally left its nest, it was ready to face the world with confidence and courage.

Like the eagle, you too can use your time alone to grow, to develop your strength and endurance, to prepare to fly.

Because at the end of the day, it's not about avoiding loneliness. It's about learning to be at ease with yourself, to enjoy your own company. It's about knowing yourself, loving yourself, respecting yourself. And once you achieve this, once you achieve this level of emotional independence, you will be able to relate to others in a healthier and more balanced way.

In his book "Solitude: A Return to the Self" (1988), psychologist and author Anthony Storr writes: "The capacity to be alone is a condition for the capacity to love." By knowing and loving oneself, we will be able to love others without dependencies, without inordinate expectations, without the need for the other to complete us. Because we will already be complete in ourselves.

So, are you ready to embrace solitude? Are you ready to face your own fears and challenges, to know yourself, to love yourself? If your answer is yes, then you are ready for the next step in your journey to emotional independence.

You may be feeling a little overwhelmed with everything we've discussed so far. That's normal. After all, you're challenging years of beliefs and thought patterns that have been with you for much of your life. But I want you to know, my friend, that every step you take on this path to emotional independence, no matter how small it may seem, is an accomplishment in itself. And I want you to be proud of it.

We have unraveled the myths of loneliness, unpacking old ideas and preconceptions to reveal the reality of what it can be: an ally, a tool for self-awareness and personal growth. We have looked at how loneliness, far from being an enemy to be feared, can be a resource for strengthening your identity and self-esteem.

Because you know what? You have the power to transform your life. You have the power to free yourself from the chains of emotional dependency. And every step you take, every belief you challenge, takes you one step closer to achieving that freedom.

Like a beautiful piece of goldsmithing, your path to emotional independence is composed of many different threads, all interwoven to create a unique work of art. So far, we have explored many of these threads: self-affirmation, self-development, self-esteem, and now, loneliness. But we still have many more to explore.

I am excited to continue this journey with you. And I hope you are too. Because what comes next is a powerful tool in your arsenal for emotional independence: assertiveness. In the next chapter, we'll explore how assertiveness can help you express your needs and desires without fear, allowing you to establish healthy, balanced relationships with others.

And remember, every time you find yourself struggling, every time you feel the old chains of emotional dependency trying to drag you back, take a deep breath, close your eyes and remind yourself that you are stronger than you think. Remind yourself that you are on this path to emotional independence because you deserve it. Because you deserve love, respect and happiness.

So, ready for the next step? Ready to continue building that masterpiece of emotional independence that is your life? Here we go! See you in the next chapter, my friend.

Chapter 13: Assertiveness: How to Express Your Needs Without Fear

Let me begin this chapter with a simple question, dear friend, have you ever had difficulty saying 'no'? Have you found it difficult to ask for what you need or want, for fear of being misunderstood or facing rejection? If so, then I encourage you to read on. In this chapter, we will delve into the wonderful and essential communication tool that is assertiveness.

Assertiveness is the foundation that allows us to establish and maintain healthy and balanced relationships, both with ourselves and with others. But what exactly is assertiveness? According to psychologist and author Albert Ellis, in his book "Assertiveness: Expression of Healthy Self-Esteem" (1990), assertiveness is defined as the ability to express our emotions, thoughts and needs in an open, honest and respectful manner, without infringing on the rights of others.

So why is it important to be assertive? Let me give you a metaphor. Imagine you are on a boat in the middle of a rough sea. The sea represents life, with its ups and downs, and your boat is your emotional well-being. Without a good navigation system, you will find yourself adrift, at the mercy of the waves. Assertiveness is like a rudder for that ship. It allows you to chart your own course, rather than being swept along by the currents.

I know it sounds complicated, but don't worry. In this chapter, we will not only understand what assertiveness is and why it is important, but we will also explore how you can develop your assertive skills. Instead of simply explaining theory, I will provide you with practical exercises and concrete examples that will help you improve your assertive communication skills.

However, before we get into the 'how to', let me tell you that assertiveness is not a skill that is acquired overnight. It is a journey, a process of continuous learning and improvement. And most importantly, every step you take on this journey, no matter how small, is an accomplishment in itself. So, are you ready to start this journey towards assertiveness?

Remember, as I mentioned in Chapter 11, assertiveness is a vital tool for self-development. And in this chapter, we will learn how assertiveness plays an essential role in that path to self-development and emotional independence.

So take a deep breath, relax and prepare to embark on this exciting journey towards more assertive and satisfying communication. Remember, you are not alone on this journey. I am here with you, as a friend, guiding you every step of the way.

And now, without further ado, let's begin our journey along the path of assertiveness!

Now that we have established what assertiveness is and why it is crucial in our lives, it is time to explore the art of being assertive in depth. As I mentioned earlier, assertiveness is not a skill that is acquired overnight. It takes practice and sometimes stepping out of our comfort zone. But I assure you that the effort is worth it. Why? Because being assertive allows you to live a life that is more authentic, fulfilling and free of unnecessary conflict. Doesn't that sound wonderful?

Assertiveness, according to Robert Alberti and Michael Emmons, in their seminal work "Your Perfect Right: Assertiveness and Equality in Your Life and Relationships" (1970), is based on two main pillars: self-assertion and respect for others. Asserting yourself means expressing your feelings and needs honestly and directly. It is giving yourself permission to say "no" when necessary, without feeling guilty. It also means recognizing and affirming your own accomplishments, abilities and value.

Respect for others, on the other hand, means recognizing and respecting the feelings and needs of others, even when they do not coincide with your own. It involves treating others with dignity and fairness, without trying to control or manipulate them.

To be assertive, it is essential to balance these two pillars. If you only assert yourself without taking into account the feelings and needs of others, you run the risk of being perceived as aggressive. On the other hand, if you only care about others without asserting yourself, you may end up being passive and not fulfilling your own needs.

Now, you may be asking yourself, how do I achieve that balance? This is where assertive communication skills come into play. These skills, which we will cover in more detail in the next section, will allow you to express your thoughts, feelings and needs effectively while maintaining respect for others.

In addition, it is important to mention that assertiveness does not only apply to interactions with others. It is also about how you treat yourself. As I mentioned in Chapter 8, understanding our own emotions is key to personal autonomy. Being assertive with yourself means being honest about your own emotions and needs, and taking steps to meet those needs in a healthy way.

Sound familiar? Chances are you're already using some of these skills in your daily life without even realizing it. And if not, don't worry. We all start somewhere, and the simple fact that you're here, reading this book and looking for ways to improve, already demonstrates your commitment to your personal growth.

So, as we continue this journey, remember to be kind to yourself. Every step, no matter how small, is a step in the right direction. And as always, I am here with you, celebrating every victory and overcoming every challenge.

Let's explore together, what exactly does it mean to balance self-affirmation and respect for others in practice? As always, reminding you that it's not about being perfect, it's about making a conscious and consistent effort. Being assertive is a journey, not a destination, and I'm here to walk you through every step of that journey.

Imagine you have a friend who asks you for a favor that you really don't want to do. Maybe he asks you to take care of his dog for the whole weekend, but you had already planned to relax and take some time for yourself. How can you handle this situation assertively?

First, acknowledging your own feelings and needs is critical. It is perfectly valid to want time for yourself and it is important to allow yourself to feel and express that. Assertive communication starts with you allowing yourself to be honest with yourself.

Once you are clear about what you feel and need, you can express it to your friend in a respectful way. This may involve saying something like, "I really appreciate you trusting me to take care of your dog. However, I've been really busy lately and need some time to myself this weekend - could we find another solution?"

Notice how in this example, not only are you expressing your needs honestly and directly, but you are also acknowledging your friend's needs and are willing to work with him to find a solution that works for both of you. That is assertiveness at its core.

On the other hand, if you chose to ignore your own needs and agree to take care of the dog, you might feel resentful and exhausted. On the other hand, if you simply told your friend "no" without offering any explanation or consideration for his needs, you could hurt his feelings and damage the relationship.

It is important to understand that assertiveness does not always guarantee that you will get what you want. Your friend may be disappointed or upset by your refusal to care for his dog. And that's okay. Assertiveness is not about controlling how others react, but about expressing yourself in a way that is in line with your values and needs.

A crucial reference on this topic is Manuel J. Smith's book "When I Say No, I Feel Guilty" (1975). Smith provides a useful guide to overcoming the feelings of guilt that can sometimes arise when we say "no". He explains that we have the right to set our own priorities and to say "no" without feeling selfish or guilty.

In addition to practical examples, assertiveness can also involve self-affirmation in terms of our abilities and accomplishments. This aspect of assertiveness is often overlooked, but it is equally important. Recognizing and affirming your own abilities and accomplishments is not boasting, but an essential part of healthy self-esteem.

It's time to ask yourself, have you been putting off your needs and desires in the name of the comfort of others? Or perhaps you've been minimizing your accomplishments, letting others hog the recognition you deserve? Or have you simply been waiting for others to read your mind, instead of clearly expressing your needs and desires? If so, you are about to embark on a transformational journey that will allow you to live a more authentic and fulfilling life.

Remember, assertiveness is a muscle. The more you exercise it, the stronger it will become. So I encourage you to practice these skills in your daily life. Try something small at first, like asking for what you really want in a restaurant, rather than settling for what you think you should ask for. Then, as you become more comfortable, you can move on to more challenging situations, such as negotiating a raise or setting boundaries in a relationship.

And don't despair if it doesn't come out perfect the first time, or the second, or even the tenth. I'm here with you every step of this journey, and I know that every effort you make brings you closer to being the most authentic and assertive version of yourself.

Just as the majestic oak tree began as a small acorn, the path to assertiveness begins with small steps. And every step you take, every time you choose to be authentic and speak your truth, you are planting the seeds of a more autonomous and empowered future.

In the next chapter, we will delve into the art of assertive communication. I will teach you practical techniques you can use to express your needs and feelings in a way that is respectful to both you and others. We will also explore how to handle criticism and conflict in an assertive manner. Because who said assertiveness is only for quiet times? Actually, it is in times of stress and conflict that our assertive skills are most needed.

Get ready to dive into an ocean of self-exploration and self-expression, and emerge with renewed confidence in yourself and your ability to navigate the waters of human interaction. Are you ready to move forward? Are you ready to become the bravest, most authentic and most assertive version of yourself? Let's get to it! Chapter 14 awaits you, full of valuable tools and techniques you can't pass up.

Chapter 14: Mindfulness and Self-understanding: The Practice of Being Present

Let us leave the past behind and return to the present, dear reader. Imagine a river, flowing with soft, gentle currents. You are in the middle of this river, observing everything around you. The sound of the water, the breeze caressing your face, the leaves dancing on the trees, the sand beneath your feet. You are aware of every little part of this moment, you are fully present. This, dear friend, is the state of mindfulness.

Mindfulness, also known as mindfulness, is an ancient practice with roots in Buddhist teachings, but don't worry, you don't need to be a Buddhist monk to practice it. In its simplest form, mindfulness is the ability to be fully present, aware of where we are and what we are doing, and not react or feel overwhelmed by what is happening around us.

Why is this relevant to our journey to freedom from emotional dependency? Well, when you experience emotional dependency, you often find yourself trapped in thoughts and emotions that keep you anchored in the past or worried about the future. This can prevent you from viewing your life and relationships objectively, which in turn can perpetuate dependent patterns of behavior.

But what if you could learn to pay attention to the present, to tune into your emotions and needs in real time, instead of getting caught in cycles of anxiety and rumination? This is what mindfulness can offer you.

In a study conducted by Keng, Smoski, and Robins in 2011, it was shown that mindfulness practice can help reduce the symptoms of emotional dependence. The reason is that mindfulness teaches us to observe our emotions and thoughts without judging them or reacting to them immediately. This gives us the opportunity to respond to our emotions in a more conscious and healthy way, instead of simply reacting automatically.

Let me ask you something, dear reader, have you ever found yourself reacting to a situation in a way that you later regretted, just because you were caught up in an avalanche of intense emotions? Wouldn't you like to have a tool that allows you to handle these moments with greater equanimity and awareness?

So, I invite you to enter this chapter with an open mind and willing to learn, to experience. Because mindfulness is not just a theory that can be understood intellectually, it is a practice that is lived in every moment. And with each moment of awareness that you cultivate, you get one step closer to emotional freedom.

So, are you ready to dive into the fascinating world of mindfulness and discover how it can help you on your path to emotional independence? Let's start this journey together!

Let us continue on our journey through the river of mindfulness. This river has a unique course, guided by the waves of your breath and the stones of your thoughts. Remember when we talked about the importance of self-affirmation in Chapter 11? How I asked you to observe your thoughts and emotions without judgment? Well, here we are again, applying those same skills. But this time, we're going a step further. Instead of simply observing, we are now learning to be fully present with our experiences.

This may seem challenging at first, and it is normal. After all, we are trying to change patterns of thinking and behavior that have been ingrained for years, perhaps even decades. But as the famous psychologist Carl Rogers said in his book "On Becoming a Person" (1961), "What remains deepest in the heart of man is often what is left out." So here we are, allowing ourselves to face what may have long been neglected.

Mindfulness meditation, a practice commonly associated with mindfulness, has its origins in ancient Buddhist teachings. But today, many psychologists and therapists around the world, such as Jon Kabat-Zinn, the founder of the Stress Reduction Clinic and the Mindfulness-Based Stress Reduction (MBSR) program at the University of Massachusetts, have adopted and adapted these techniques to help people manage everything from stress and anxiety to emotional dependency.

Kabat-Zinn, in his book "Full Catastrophe Living" (1990), defines mindfulness as "the awareness that arises from paying attention, intentionally, to the present moment, without judgment." It is this "non-judgmental" component that I believe can be especially helpful for those of us who struggle with emotional dependency.

Often, people with emotional dependency can be extremely hard on themselves, full of self-criticism and judgment. However, mindfulness teaches us to observe our experiences without judgment. Instead of judging yourself for feeling a certain way, you simply notice the emotion. You recognize that it is there. You accept it. And then, you can decide how you want to respond to it.

Remember, my friend, there are no "bad" or "good" emotions. There are only emotions. And they are all valid parts of the human experience. So the next time you find yourself in the midst of a surge of intense emotions, I invite you to practice mindfulness. Notice your emotions. Allow yourself to feel. And then choose how you want to respond.

Are you ready to dive deeper into the river of mindfulness? Go ahead, the water is great!

Now that we've talked about the meaning and importance of mindfulness, how does it actually apply in everyday life? To answer this question, let's allow our feet to dip into the waters of mindfulness once again.

Remember when in Chapter 3 we discussed how emotional dependency can make you feel like you're strapped into a roller coaster of emotions, constantly going up and down with no control over where the ride takes you? Mindfulness practice can be that calm breeze that helps you keep your feet on the ground, even when the ride gets turbulent.

A practical example of this can be the practice of mindfulness meditation. In his book "The Miracle of Mindfulness" (1975), the famous Buddhist monk Thich Nhat Hanh describes a simple mindfulness meditation technique that can be practiced anywhere, anytime. It simply involves paying attention to your breathing.

Imagine this: you are sitting in your favorite spot in the house, perhaps in front of a window with a nice view. Your eyes are closed and your hands are resting gently on your legs. You concentrate on your breathing, noticing how the air moves in and out of your lungs. You don't try to control your breathing in any way; you simply observe it, just as it is.

When you realize that your mind has begun to wander, as it often does, simply notice that this has happened and then gently turn your attention back to your breathing. There is no need to judge yourself for letting your mind wander. Remember, mindfulness is about observation, not judgment.

This type of meditation may seem incredibly simple, but its effectiveness is profound. As Thich Nhat Hanh pointed out, "The true realization of meditation comes with practice in daily life." This means that not only can you practice mindfulness during a formal meditation, but you can also practice it at any time during the day.

You could practice mindfulness while eating, focusing on the tastes, textures and smells of your food. You could practice it while walking, paying attention to the sensations of your feet touching the ground. You could even practice it while doing everyday chores like washing the dishes or watering the plants.

The trick is to begin to see every moment as an opportunity to practice mindfulness. And when you regularly practice mindfulness, you can begin to notice a shift in your relationship with your emotions and your thoughts. Instead of being swept along by the current, you can learn to surf the waves with grace and balance.

So how about taking a step further into the waters of mindfulness? After all, my friend, you never know what treasures you may discover in the depths of your own being.

And so, together, we have explored the wondrous waters of mindfulness and self-understanding. As we have delved deeper into its understanding, we have discovered its ability to bring us to a place of peace and balance. We have learned that it is more than just a passing fad; it is a valuable tool that allows us to open ourselves to the experience of the present moment in a way that is both compassionate and non-judgmental.

Together, we recalled the wise words of Thich Nhat Hanh and how he encourages us to integrate mindfulness into every moment of our daily lives. In addition, we learned to appreciate the importance of mindfulness meditation and how it helps us build a healthy relationship with our emotions and thoughts.

Perhaps, in the process of this journey, you have felt a little uncomfortable. It could be the first time that you are really opening up to your thoughts and feelings, without trying to change them, analyze them or judge them. It can be disconcerting at first, but remember, this is perfectly normal. In fact, it's a sign that you're making real progress on your journey toward freedom from emotional dependency.

We're navigating uncharted territory together, and that can be daunting at times. But remember, you are not in this alone. I am here with you, my friend, and together we can learn to navigate the shifting currents of human experience with grace, courage and compassion.

As we prepare for the next chapter of our journey, I want you to remember something. Remember that the road to emotional freedom is not a sprint, but a marathon. It's not about getting to the finish line quickly, it's about maintaining a steady, sustained pace. It's about cultivating patience, compassion and self-understanding, and allowing yourself to move forward at your own pace.

In the next chapter, we will explore one of the most powerful forces in the universe: self-love. We will learn how self-love is not just a buzz phrase, but a life force that drives emotional independence. So close your eyes, take a deep breath and get ready to embark on a life-changing journey.

Keep hope alive, my friend. Together, we are taking important steps toward liberation from emotional dependency. I look forward to seeing you in the next chapter, with the promise of new discoveries, new wisdom and new ways of being in the world. See you there.

Chapter 15: Self-Love: The Force Driving Emotional Independence

Dear reader, if you have made it this far, I congratulate you on the road you have traveled. We know it has not been easy, but I am sure you have picked up every teaching with openness and determination. And now, here we are, ready to enter the heart of liberation from emotional dependence: self-love.

Why is self-esteem so important? Let me ask you this question: Remember when we talked in Chapter 2 about the crucial role of self-esteem in emotional dependence? Self-love is the key to strengthening our self-esteem and, therefore, is fundamental to conquering emotional independence.

Understanding self-love is like meeting an old friend who has always been by your side, but who you may have forgotten in the hustle and bustle of life. It is a process of self-discovery and re-discovery, of reconciliation and healing.

But make no mistake, cultivating self-love is no easy task. In a world that often encourages us to seek external approval and compare ourselves to others, learning to love ourselves can be a significant challenge. But I assure you, it is a challenge worth facing. Did you know that a lack of self-love has been associated with an increased risk of depression, anxiety, and stress (Sowislo & Orth, 2013). So this journey we are about to embark on is not only to free ourselves from emotional dependency, but also to improve our overall mental health.

Are you ready to discover the power of self-love? Are you ready to embark on this journey that will allow you to connect with yourself in a deeper and more authentic way? I promise that, by the end of this chapter, you will have a new understanding of what it means to love yourself and how this unconditional love for yourself can be the driving force behind your emotional independence.

As we explore self-love, I invite you to open yourself to the possibilities. You may find some of the ideas and concepts we will discuss new or even challenging. But remember, we are here to learn and grow together. So, if you're ready, let's take a deep breath, open our hearts and embark on this exciting journey into self-love.

Because, as the Greek philosopher and poet Epicurus once said: "Of all the things that wisdom provides to achieve complete happiness throughout life, the possession of friendship is by far the most important" (Epicurus, Letters, Doctrines and Fragments, 3rd century B.C.). And on this occasion, I invite you to discover the most vital friendship of all, the one you have with yourself. Are you ready? Let's begin.

To truly understand self-esteem, it is useful to distinguish it from self-esteem, although the two are closely related. Self-esteem, as we have already mentioned in previous chapters, has to do with how you value yourself, your perception of your worth as an individual. Self-love, on the other hand, is an unconditional affection for yourself. It is the acceptance of who you are, with all your strengths and weaknesses, your triumphs and your mistakes.

Author and psychotherapist Nathaniel Branden, known as the "father of self-esteem," wrote in his work "The Six Pillars of Self-Esteem" (1994) that self-love is the foundation for a full and satisfying life. According to Branden, when we love someone, we value that person. So, if we love ourselves, we value ourselves. Do you realize how powerful self-love can be?

I cannot fail to mention another great figure, professor and researcher Brené Brown. In her book "The Gift of Imperfection" (2010), Brown defines self-love as "the practice of treating ourselves with kindness and understanding when we fail or make mistakes, rather than ignoring our pains or flagellating ourselves with self-criticism." Brown reminds us that we are all human, and as humans, we are subject to mistakes and failures. But instead of punishing ourselves for these mistakes, self-love invites us to accept and care for ourselves in these difficult moments.

So how do we cultivate self-love? Just like a plant that needs water, light and nutrients to grow, self-love needs our attention, understanding and patience.

First, we must acknowledge our emotions and feelings. This may sound simple, but in a society that often teaches us to suppress our emotions, it can be a difficult task. Remember in Chapter 8 when we talked about understanding our emotions? Those learnings are essential here. By acknowledging our emotions, we are validating our experiences and accepting our humanity.

Second, we need to practice self-compassion. Self-compassion is being kind and compassionate to yourself, especially in times of pain or failure. Instead of harshly criticizing yourself, you treat yourself with the same kindness and understanding that you would give to a good friend in a similar situation. Self-love is not arrogance or narcissism, it is kindness and compassion toward yourself.

Are you ready to embark on this exciting journey of self-discovery and self-love? Because now is the time, my friend, to give yourself permission to love yourself and value yourself for who you are. And remember, every step, no matter how small, is a step towards emotional independence.

Continuing our journey, let us now talk about concrete examples. How does self-love manifest itself in daily life? How does it look and feel? How does it live?

Imagine someone, let's call her Laura, who works in a high-pressure environment where mistakes are not tolerated and failure is seen as a weakness. One day, Laura makes a mistake on an important project. Instead of falling into self-criticism and shame, Laura allows herself to feel her emotions: disappointment, frustration, fear. She recognizes that she has made a mistake, but she also recognizes that she is human and that mistakes are a natural part of life. Instead of beating herself up, Laura takes time to take care of herself, perhaps by taking a relaxing bath or going for a walk in nature. This is a manifestation of self-love in action.

Another example might be a young man, let's call him David, who has grown up in a family where emotions were not welcome. David has learned to suppress his feelings and present a facade of "being okay" all the time. But David decides he wants to break this pattern. He begins attending therapy, where he learns to recognize and express his emotions. He begins to allow himself to feel, even when the emotions are uncomfortable or painful. David also begins to practice meditation, which helps him cultivate self-compassion and be present in the moment. David is actively cultivating his self-love.

These are just two examples, but there are infinite ways in which self-love can manifest itself in our daily lives. The important thing to remember is that self-love is not a destination, but a journey. It is not about reaching a state of perfection, but learning to embrace our imperfection with kindness and compassion.

Self-love does not mean that you never feel sad, angry or scared. Self-love means that you allow yourself to feel all of your emotions, and treat yourself with kindness and compassion, regardless of what you are feeling. As Brené Brown reminded us, self-love is "the practice of treating ourselves with kindness and understanding when we fail or make mistakes, rather than ignoring our pains or flagellating ourselves with self-criticism."

To close this section, I invite you to do a little exercise. Think of a recent situation in which you made a mistake or felt bad about yourself. How did you treat yourself at that moment? With criticism or with kindness? What could you do differently next time? Remember, every step, no matter how small, is a step toward self-love and emotional independence.

Now that we've explored the essence of self-love and I've shown you how it manifests in everyday life, you may be asking yourself, "So now what, how can I start cultivating self-love in my own life?" Well, that's exactly what we're going to talk about now.

Developing self-esteem can be an intimidating process at first. You may feel resistance or even fear. And that's okay. It's completely normal. Self-love is a journey, not a destination. It's not about getting to a place where you suddenly love yourself unconditionally. It's about making small choices every day that reflect your commitment to treating yourself with kindness and respect.

There are numerous strategies and techniques you can use to cultivate self-love. Some people find meditation or mindfulness helpful. Others may prefer therapy or coaching. Some people like to write in a journal, or practice yoga, or spend time in nature. There is no single answer. The important thing is to find what works for you.

A good place to start may be to simply take a few moments each day to tune into yourself. You can ask yourself, "How am I feeling today, how can I take care of myself right now?" Another helpful strategy can be self-compassion, which is the practice of treating yourself with the same kindness and care you would give to a good friend.

See how it all intertwines? The concepts from the previous chapters, such as mindfulness, self-affirmation and self-understanding, are all fundamental pieces of this journey toward self-love. Each contributes to building a stronger, more resilient self, a self that is able to withstand the storms of life without being swept away by them.

The path to self-love is one of the most rewarding and transformative journeys you can take. And although it won't always be easy, I assure you it's worth it.

And now, we are ready to move into the next chapter of our journey: changing beliefs. Remember how much we talked about the importance of beliefs and thought patterns in the previous chapters? Well, now we're going to take it a step further. We're going to explore how you can actively change those beliefs and thought patterns that don't serve you. I promise it will be an eye-opening and liberating journey.

But before we get into that exciting journey, I want you to take a moment to recognize how far you've come. Look at yourself with eyes of gratitude and appreciation. And always remember, you are worthy of love and respect, no matter what. You, my dear reader, are incredibly valuable, simply for being you. And I hope that every day you are one step closer to recognizing that truth for yourself.

See you in the next chapter, my friend. I assure you that you won't want to miss it. see you soon!

Chapter 16: Changing Beliefs: Reconstructing Thought for Emotional Freedom

If you have made it this far, my friend, it means that you have demonstrated an enormous commitment to your personal growth. I congratulate you. You've come a long way, delving into the labyrinth of your psyche, unlocking the secrets of your emotional dependency, discovering how to nurture your self-esteem, exploring your emotions, affirming your identity, embracing the power of self-love.... Quite a journey, don't you think? And yet, we have not yet reached the end. On the contrary, we are about to embark on one of the most important steps of this journey: changing our beliefs.

Why is it so important to change our beliefs, you ask? Well, let me tell you something: our beliefs are the skeleton of our reality. They are the glasses through which we interpret the world. The beliefs we harbor in our minds are powerful, so powerful that they can determine our actions, our feelings, even our sense of identity. If our beliefs are distorted or harmful, then our world can become distorted and harmful.

Remember when we talked about self-esteem in Chapter 2? We talked about how low self-esteem can be the breeding ground for emotional dependency. Well, here's where things get really interesting. Because low self-esteem doesn't come out of nowhere. It feeds on beliefs. Beliefs about ourselves, beliefs about others, beliefs about the world.

For example, you may have an ingrained belief that says, "I'm not enough." Or perhaps, "No one will love me if I don't do what they want." Or even, "If someone leaves me, that means

I'm worthless." These beliefs can be enormously destructive. They can make you feel trapped in patterns of behavior and thinking that lead you again and again to emotional dependency.

Now, the problem is not having beliefs. We all have them. The problem is when our beliefs do not serve us. When they cause us pain, instead of bringing us peace. When they make us feel lesser, instead of reminding us of our immense worth. And that's where belief change comes in.

Think of your beliefs as the roots of a tree. If the tree is diseased, it doesn't make sense to just prune the branches. You need to go deeper. You need to get to the root of the problem. And that's exactly what we're going to do in this chapter. We're going to dive into the fertile soil of your mind, we're going to explore the roots of your beliefs and we're going to learn how to change them.

I am excited to embark on this journey with you, dear reader. Are you ready? Are you willing to question your beliefs, to challenge them, to change them? Are you willing to break free from the chains that bind you and embrace a new vision of yourself and the world?

Excellent! I see that light of determination in your eyes. And so, we continued our exploration.

Our journey now takes us into the fascinating field of cognitive psychology. Albert Ellis, a leading cognitive psychologist, creator of Rational Emotive Behavioral Therapy (REBT), claimed that our emotions and behaviors are the product of our beliefs, not directly the events that happen to us. Can you see the transformational potential in this? "If you change your beliefs, you change your life," Ellis said.

Accompanying him, Aaron T. Beck, the father of cognitive therapy, asserted that people suffering from depression, anxiety and other psychological disorders are often trapped in a series of negative, self-defeating beliefs. His revolutionary cognitive therapy is based on helping people question and change these beliefs.

But how can we change our beliefs? How can we unravel these deep-rooted thought patterns that seem to be part of us?

This is where self-observation comes into play, that powerful tool we have already discussed in previous chapters. You have to become an attentive observer of your own mind. You have to notice your thoughts, your feelings, your reactions. You have to learn to recognize the beliefs that underlie your thought patterns and behavior.

Now, this is not easy. At first, it may seem like trying to see the air. But with practice, patience and kindness to yourself, you will begin to see the subtle currents of thought flowing in your mind.

And remember, you are not in this alone. You can seek the help of a professional, a therapist or counselor who is familiar with cognitive therapy. But even without outside help, you can begin to do this work on your own. You can begin to become aware of your thoughts and beliefs.

So I invite you to start doing it now. Observe your thoughts. Notice the beliefs that are operating in your mind. Do it with curiosity, without judgment. As if you were an adventurous explorer venturing into new territory.

Do you find it difficult? Don't worry, that's normal. You are learning a new skill. Let me give you a practical example of how to do it.

Imagine you've had a bad day at work. Your boss has scolded you and you're feeling down. Instead of letting negative thoughts drag you down, stop for a moment. Look at your thoughts. What are you saying to yourself? Maybe you're thinking, "I'm a failure. I can't do anything right." These are beliefs. And they are beliefs you can question and change.

Now, changing beliefs does not mean simply replacing a negative thought with a positive one. It is not that simple. Changing beliefs involves deep questioning, a thorough review of the evidence, an examination of your value system and convictions.

You can start by asking yourself, "Is there real evidence that I am a failure just because my boss scolded me? Does a one-time event define who I am as a person? Couldn't it be that I simply made a mistake, just like any human being?" Let me tell you something, my friend, making mistakes is a human thing, we all make them. Mistakes are opportunities to learn and grow, not definitive judgments of our worth.

So the next time you find yourself stuck in a negative thought, stop for a moment. Look at that thought. Is it really true, or is it simply an ingrained belief that you have accepted without question?

And this is where another powerful tool comes into play: cognitive restructuring. This term may sound complicated, but the idea is simple. It's about challenging and changing our irrational or self-defeating beliefs. Cognitive restructuring is a central part of cognitive therapy and has been shown to be very effective in treating a variety of psychological problems, including emotional dependency.

So how exactly does cognitive restructuring work? Let's look at a practical example.

Suppose you have the belief that "if I don't make my partner happy, I am not worthy of being loved". This is a destructive belief that can feed emotional dependency. How could you restructure this belief?

You could start by questioning it. Is it really true that your value as a person depends on how happy you make your partner? Isn't it more realistic to think that everyone is responsible for their own happiness? Isn't it possible to be worthy of love even if you can't satisfy all of your partner's needs?

Then you could look for evidence that contradicts your belief. Maybe there are times when you have not been able to make your partner happy, but they still loved you. Maybe there are people in your life who love you for who you are, not for what you do for them.

Finally, you could replace your destructive belief with a healthier, more realistic one. Something like, "My value as a person does not depend on making my partner happy. I am worthy of love just the way I am."

This is just one example, of course. Cognitive restructuring can be a challenging process and requires practice. But with time and dedication, it can be a tremendously effective tool for changing our beliefs and freeing us from emotional dependency.

And again, you are not alone in this process. There are many tools and resources available to help you. From books and courses to therapists and support groups. Remember, in Chapter 18 we'll delve more deeply into support networks and how they can help you on your path to emotional independence.

So, what do you say we get down to business, are you ready to challenge your beliefs and open the door to a new reality, one where you are free, independent and full of self-love? Remember, it's not an easy road but believe me when I tell you, it's an absolutely worthwhile journey.

Remember, changing beliefs does not happen overnight. It takes time, patience and persistence. Just as you can't build a house in a day, you can't change an ingrained belief in an instant. But, my friend, don't you think it's worth investing in the home of your thoughts?

However, it is not only important to question our beliefs and reconstruct them. It is also crucial to consider what new beliefs we want to bring into our lives. These new beliefs must be empowering, affirming and, above all, they must resonate with you.

For example, a new belief might be, "I have the right to express my feelings and needs." Or "I am in charge of my own happiness." Or perhaps "I am enough, just the way I am." These are just suggestions, of course. You have the power to decide what beliefs you want in your life. You are the architect of your own mind.

Throughout this chapter, we have explored the crucial role our beliefs play in our lives. We have discussed how our beliefs, both conscious and unconscious, can fuel emotional dependency and have explored how we can change those beliefs to free ourselves from the chains of dependency.

But remember, this is just one step on your journey to emotional freedom. And you are not alone. I'm here with you, my friend, every step of the way. And I'm excited to see where this journey takes you.

You may be wondering, "And after all this work on changing my beliefs, what's next? How do I handle the challenges that life will inevitably throw at me?" Good news, dear reader, that's the topic of our next chapter, "Tools for Resilience Development."

In the next chapter, we will explore resilience, that incredible internal resource that allows us to face adversity, adapt, learn and grow. We will understand how to develop this skill and how it can be your ally on the road to emotional independence.

Let me give you a preview: Resilience is not something you either have or don't have. It's a skill that can be cultivated, and in the next chapter I'll show you how.

Are you ready to continue this journey? Are you excited to discover more tools and strategies to strengthen your emotional independence? I promise it will be an exciting journey, full of discovery and growth. See you in Chapter 17, my friend.

But for now, take a moment to reflect on what we have discussed in this chapter. Ask yourself questions. Question your beliefs. And always remember, you are on the right path, the path to your emotional freedom. Until the next chapter, I send you a big hug and all my support on your journey.

Chapter 17: Tools for Resilience Development

We are in the midst of a transcendental journey. We have excavated our emotions, uncovered our limiting beliefs and rebuilt our self-love, all while learning to be more assertive and aware. But what prepares us for the challenges to come? How do we equip ourselves for life's inevitable trials and tribulations? This is where resilience comes in.

Resilience is not just a buzzword in the field of personal development and psychology. It is a critical skill, an invisible shield that protects you in difficult times and allows you to bounce back stronger and wiser after each blow. It is not an innate characteristic, exclusive to a few lucky people, but an ability that we can all cultivate with time and practice.

But what exactly is resilience? Simply put, resilience is the ability to adapt and recover from adversity. But, I assure you, it is much more than that. Resilience is an inner strength that allows us to handle stress, overcome personal and professional difficulties, and move forward despite obstacles.

Now, dear reader, I would like to ask you a question: Do you consider yourself a resilient person? Why or why not? This is a question to reflect on, to really dive into the essence of what it means to be resilient.

Psychologists have identified several factors that contribute to resilience. These include having positive relationships, the ability to make realistic plans and carry them out, a positive view of oneself, skills in managing emotions, and problem-solving skills.

You may be thinking, "This all sounds great, but how do I build my resilience?" Well, I'm glad you asked, because that's exactly what we're going to talk about in this chapter.

Before we dive into tools and techniques for developing resilience, I would like to mention an inspirational quote from Viktor Frankl, author of the book "Man's Search for Meaning" (1946). Frankl, a psychiatrist and Holocaust survivor, wrote: "When we are no longer able to change a situation, we face the challenge of changing ourselves." This quote encapsulates the essence of resilience: the ability to adapt and grow despite difficult circumstances.

So, my friend, let's go into the vast world of resilience. We're in for a fascinating journey, full of revelations and discoveries, and I'm happy to join you every step of the way. So fasten your seatbelt and get ready to explore how you can equip yourself with the invisible armor of resilience.

We are halfway through this chapter, our journey toward strengthening resilience. Each step, each new concept is a brick that contributes to building our emotional strength. You are an architect, slowly building your own castle of resilience. Isn't that exciting?

In 1989, psychologist Emmy Werner conducted a study of children on the island of Kauai in Hawaii. What she discovered was truly eye-opening. Despite growing up in unfavorable conditions, one-third of the children studied thrived in adulthood. Their secret? Resilience. According to Werner, these children demonstrated "a capacity for planning and goal selection, faith in their own efficacy, and a consistent willingness to seek support from others." His study, described in detail in his book Vulnerable but Invincible: The High-Risk Children of Hawaii (1992), underscores the importance of resilience in overcoming adversity.

To cultivate resilience, we need some tools. No, you don't need a hammer or a screwdriver, although sometimes you might feel like you'd like to hit some obstacles that get in your way. These tools are strategies, mindsets and techniques that you can apply in your daily life. Let's explore some of them.

First, practicing mindfulness can be extremely helpful. If you have been following this book from the beginning, you will already be familiar with this practice from chapter 14. Mindfulness allows you to become more aware of your thoughts and emotions without being swept away by them. By learning to observe your experiences without judgment, you can gain valuable perspective and decrease the intensity of negative emotions.

But how do you practice mindfulness in the midst of an emotional storm? Well, imagine you are in the ocean, the waves churning around you. Your thoughts and emotions are the waves, unpredictable and powerful. But with mindfulness, instead of fighting the waves, you learn to float on them, to observe them and let them pass.

Next on our list of tools is self-compassion. Psychologist Kristin Neff, author of "Self-Compassion: The Power of Being Kind to Yourself" (2011), defines self-compassion as the ability to treat yourself with the same kindness and understanding that you would treat a good friend. When faced with difficult situations, self-compassion allows you to give yourself a break, recognizing that we all struggle and make mistakes.

Finally, cultivating a growth mindset can be a great help. According to Carol Dweck, author of "Mindset: The Attitude of Success" (2006), people with a growth mindset believe that they can develop their skills and abilities through effort and dedication.

So how does this growth mindset apply to resilience? Imagine you're in a stressful situation. Your boss has given you harsh feedback, your partner has had a bad day and taken it out on you, your car has broken down on the way to an important appointment. Instead of despairing and telling yourself, "I can't handle this," you can say, "This is a challenge, but I'm learning and growing from this experience." In this way, every challenge becomes an opportunity to strengthen your resilience.

Of course, adopting a growth mindset doesn't mean ignoring your feelings or pretending that everything is okay when it's not. In fact, it's quite the opposite. It means acknowledging your emotions, allowing yourself to feel, and then asking yourself, "What can I learn from this? How can I grow from this?" And that, dear reader, is the superpower of the growth mindset.

Now, let's move on to some concrete examples. Remember, these are simply illustrations of how you might apply these tools in your daily life. Each person is unique, and what works for one may not work for another.

Imagine you've moved to a new city for work. You're excited, but also nervous. You miss your home, your friends, the familiarity of your old life, and change is hard, we know. Change is hard, we know. How can you apply mindfulness in this situation? Instead of letting yourself get carried away with homesickness and anxiety, you could take a few moments to sit quietly and observe your emotions. What does that homesickness feel like in your body? And the anxiety? By observing them without judgment, you may find that they are less overwhelming than you thought.

In the same situation, you could apply self-compassion by acknowledging that what you are going through is difficult. You can give yourself permission to feel sad, to be homesick. There's nothing wrong with that. As Kristin Neff says, "Self-compassion involves being kind to yourself in times of pain or failure rather than ignoring our sufferings or flagellating ourselves with self-criticism."

And finally, you could apply a growth mindset by looking at this situation as a growth opportunity. Yes, it's challenging. Yes, it's unfamiliar. But it's also an opportunity to learn new skills, meet new people and discover new places. Every day is a new adventure, a new lesson.

Tools such as mindfulness, self-compassion and a growth mindset can be extraordinarily helpful on your path to resilience. But remember, dear reader, it's not about being perfect. It's not about never feeling pain, sadness or fear. It's about learning to dance with them, to embrace them as part of your human experience.

So, are you ready to continue your journey?

Are you ready to embrace challenge, change, uncertainty with a smile on your face and determination in your heart? That's resilience, dear reader, and I'm here to tell you that you have the power to cultivate it within yourself.

By reminding you that you are not alone in this, I hope you will be comforted. We all, to varying degrees and at various times in our lives, face adversity that tests our emotional fortitude. But we also all have the capacity to learn, grow and overcome those trials. So do you.

When you face adversity, remember that you are like the reed that bends but does not break. You are flexible, adaptable, able to withstand even the fiercest storms. And even though you may feel knocked down at times, you always have the ability to get up and keep going.

Your resilience is not measured by how many times you fall down, but by how many times you get up. Isn't that really inspiring? Life can be hard, it can be challenging, but it can also be an incredible opportunity to learn and grow. And therein lies the beauty of resilience.

Now, as we prepare to move into the next chapter, I promise you that even more fascinating discoveries await us. As we continue our journey, we will learn about how to cultivate a positive mindset, a powerful ally in our journey to resilience. We will explore the science of positivity, how it affects our brain and body, and how we can integrate it into our daily lives.

We will learn how to change our thought patterns, how to replace negative thoughts with positive ones, and how this change can have a profound impact on our happiness and well-being. All this and much more awaits you in the next chapter.

So, dear reader, I invite you to go ahead. Together, we can explore the deepest recesses of our minds and discover the strength that lies within. Are you ready for the next step in this exciting journey? Until then, remember, you are stronger than you think and more resilient than you believe. Let's see how far that power can take us.

Chapter 18: The Power of Support Networks on the Road to Freedom

Have you ever had that drowning feeling, that you are sinking and need a hand to pull you up? Or perhaps, an impulse that motivates you to keep going when you seem to be trapped in the dark? Have you felt the need for someone who understands what you are going through, who supports you, advises you, listens to you? You are not alone in this, my dear reader. We all need support at certain times in our lives. We all need an environment that makes us feel understood, valued, respected and loved. And this need is perfectly normal and human.

What's more, it is healthy and essential to our emotional well-being. We cannot underestimate the power of a strong support network in our lives. It is that support network that gives us the strength to keep going when everything seems to be falling apart. The one that reminds us that we are stronger than we think we are. The one that inspires us to be the best version of ourselves.

But what exactly is a support network, and how can it contribute to our freedom from emotional dependency?

A support network is not simply a group of people. It is a system made up of individuals who provide you with emotional, psychological and sometimes even physical help. They can be family members, friends, colleagues, therapists, self-help groups, even your pets. The people who are part of your support network understand you, listen to you and provide you with the help you need.

According to psychologist Susan Pinker, in her work "The Village Effect" (2014), strong and supportive social relationships can have a huge impact on our health and longevity. In her book, Pinker addresses the importance of human connection for mental and physical health, happiness and longevity. He asserts that strong social relationships and community support can not only help us live longer, but also live better.

Think about it for a moment. How do you feel when you are with people who understand, support and respect you? Do you notice a relief, a sense of acceptance, a surge of love and gratitude? That's exactly what a support network provides: a safe environment where you can be yourself, express your emotions, your fears, your hopes and your dreams. A place where you can fall and get up, where you can learn and grow.

On our path to freedom from emotional dependency, a strong support network can be our greatest ally. Not only does it provide us with a shoulder to cry on, but it also provides us with a mirror in which we can see ourselves clearly and objectively. It helps us understand that we are not alone in our journey, that there are people who care about us, and that we are connected to the world in a deeper and more meaningful way.

Continuing in this vein, let me ask you, dear reader: Have you ever reflected on the quality of the people who make up your current support network? Are they people who truly understand, respect and value you for who you are? Are they individuals who encourage you to grow and develop, or do they keep you trapped in negative cycles and patterns of emotional dependency? It is essential to be honest with yourself and evaluate the quality of our relationships.

Sometimes, it may be that the people we think of as supportive are actually feeding our emotional dependency. They could be people who, because of their own insecurity or fear, keep us in unfulfilling roles and relationships. Or perhaps they are people who unwittingly reinforce us in patterns of dependency because of their own unresolved struggles.

This does not mean that we should cut those people out of our lives. We are all human, we all have our struggles and no one is perfect. However, it does mean that we may need to expand our support network and incorporate new relationships and healthy connections. As philosopher and poet Ralph Waldo Emerson said in his famous essay "Friendship" (1841), "The only way to have a friend is to be one." This implies that we need to be selective about who we allow into our lives and how those people influence our personal growth and our freedom from emotional dependency.

It is important to remember that healthy support networks are not created overnight. They take time, effort and commitment. It is not a matter of quantity, but of quality. It's not about having a large number of "friends," it's about having people who genuinely support, understand and encourage you on your journey.

In this sense, an effective support network must be able to offer you a variety of perspectives and experiences. It must be able to challenge and encourage you to continue to grow and learn. It must be a safe space where you can express yourself freely, share your fears, your dreams, your failures and your successes.

This reminds me of what Brene Brown, famous professor and researcher, said in her work "The Power of Vulnerability" (2012). Brown highlights the importance of vulnerability in our relationships and how it allows us to connect deeply with others. She explains that to allow ourselves to be vulnerable, we need to feel safe, valued and respected. We need to know that we will not be judged or criticized for our struggles and that our experiences will be acknowledged and understood.

This is how an effective support network can act as a powerful catalyst on our path to freedom from emotional dependency. It offers us a safe space in which we can authentically be ourselves, explore our emotions and thoughts, face our fears and overcome our challenges. It reminds us that we are not alone in our journey and that every step we take on this path is a step towards freedom and personal growth.

Now, let me illustrate with an example how this support network can work. Imagine you are in a dark forest, full of uncertainty and fear. Emotional dependency is that darkness that envelops you, that doesn't let you see clearly, that makes you feel lost and trapped. But then, in the distance, you see a small flickering light. You approach it and discover that it is a small lit torch. When you pick it up, the light expands and allows you to see a little further. That torch is your first friend, the one who is always there for you, who understands and supports you.

But the road is long and the light of a single torch is not enough to light the whole way. So as you go along, you find more torches, each bringing its own light and warmth. Some torches are larger and brighter, others are smaller and dimmer, but all are important and all contribute to lighting your path. These torches are the members of your support network, each with their own light and warmth, each contributing to your path to freedom from emotional dependency.

Do you see how powerful it can be to have a strong support network? Not only does it provide you with light and warmth in the midst of darkness, but it also gives you the strength and courage to move forward, to explore the forest, to face your fears and overcome your challenges.

Psychologist Carl Rogers, in his work "On Becoming a Person" (1961), emphasized the importance of having an environment of acceptance and understanding for personal growth. According to Rogers, only when we feel accepted and understood can we explore and understand our emotions and thoughts, and thus begin our journey towards emotional growth and autonomy.

This is precisely the function of a support network: to provide an environment of acceptance and understanding in which we can explore and understand our emotions and thoughts, face our fears and overcome our challenges.

Now, dear reader, I ask you: Do you feel that you have an environment of acceptance and understanding around you? Do you have people who support you, encourage you and help you overcome your challenges? Or do you feel isolated, misunderstood and trapped in your emotional dependency?

Don't be afraid to seek support. Don't be afraid to expand your network. Don't be afraid to ask for help. Remember, we all need a little help on our journey. We all need a little light to illuminate our path. We all need a helping hand to pick us up when we fall. So don't be afraid to seek that help, to seek that light, to seek that helping hand. Because ultimately, you are not in this alone. We are on this journey together, and together we can overcome any challenge that comes our way.

Delving even deeper into this concept, psychologist and author Brené Brown, in her work "Daring Greatly" (2012), advocates the power of vulnerability and how this act of bravery can open the door to deeper and more meaningful human connections. That is the essence of a support network: it is based on vulnerability and authenticity.

So, my dear reader, I invite you to be brave. I invite you to be vulnerable and to seek authentic connections. I invite you to surround yourself with people who support you, understand you and encourage you on your path to emotional independence.

You may now be asking yourself, how do you build a support network? Well, every network is unique and is built according to individual needs and interests. But there are always some universal guidelines that can help you in this process. It can be finding a support group of people who are going through similar situations, or it can be a therapist or counselor to guide you in your personal growth process. It can also be your family, friends, co-workers or neighbors. The important thing is that you feel that these people understand you, support you and help you grow.

Remember that building a support network does not happen overnight. It is a process that takes time, patience and effort. But I guarantee it's worth it. Because when you have a solid support network, you have a foundation on which you can build your emotional independence.

Are you already visualizing your own network? Can you see those friendly faces that help you keep the torch of your autonomy burning?

In closing, I hope this chapter has given you a new perspective on the power and importance of support networks on the road to emotional independence. I have given you a preview of how support networks can be the light in the midst of the darkness, they can be the torches that help light your way and give you the strength to move forward.

In the next chapter, we will delve into an equally crucial topic: healthy relationships. For, after all, what is a support network if not a collection of healthy relationships? And how can we identify, cultivate, and maintain these healthy relationships in our lives? How can they help us overcome emotional dependency and build our emotional autonomy?

That's what we'll explore in the next chapter. So get ready, because this journey still has many fascinating things to discover. And remember, on this journey you are not alone. You have your support network, you have this book, and you have me, your traveling companion, always ready to light the way.

I invite you to go ahead, to take the next step on this road to emotional independence. I promise you it will be worth it.

Chapter 19: Healthy Relationships: What They Are and How to Build Them

Dear reader, we are here once again, embracing this path of self-knowledge and personal growth together. If you have made it this far, it is because you have demonstrated your steadfastness, your courage and your commitment to your emotional health. Now, emotional independence seems much less of a distant goal and more of a tangible possibility, don't you think?

Now, we come to a key point in our journey, an essential element for anyone seeking to break free from the chains of emotional dependency: healthy relationships. Of all the lessons we are learning together, this may be one of the most important. Why? Because relationships directly affect our mental, emotional and even physical health. But what exactly are healthy relationships and how do we build them? That, my dear reader, is what we are going to explore in this chapter.

Let's dive together into the wonderful world of healthy relationships, where every interaction is an opportunity for growth, genuine connection and unconditional love. And no, I'm not just talking about romantic relationships, but about all the relationships in our lives, from our family and friends to our colleagues and acquaintances.

But what makes a relationship healthy? How can we know if we are in a healthy relationship or one that is hurting us? And perhaps the most important question: how can we build and maintain healthy relationships in our lives? Have you ever asked yourself these questions? If so, this chapter is for you.

Healthy relationships are based on a set of fundamental principles that make them work, that make them nurturing and enriching. Dr. Lisa Firestone, in her book "Conquering Your Critical Inner Voice" (2002), describes some of these essential characteristics: mutual respect, honesty, open communication, trust, equality and mutual support. But there is something else that all healthy relationships have in common, and that is self-love.

Sounds simple, doesn't it? But the truth is that these principles require practice and effort. They require us to know ourselves, to love ourselves, and to be able to set boundaries and ask for what we need.

And here's the big paradox: to have healthy relationships, we first need to be emotionally independent. Remember what we discussed in Chapter 10 about rebuilding the autonomous self? To establish genuine, healthy connections with others, we must first have a solid, healthy relationship with ourselves. For only when we are comfortable with ourselves, when we love and respect ourselves, can we love and respect others in the same way.

Now, knowing what we know, it is time to do a little exercise of introspection. How are the relationships in your life today? Do they comply with these fundamental principles of healthy relationships that we have just described? Are they spaces where you feel respected, loved, supported and free to be yourself? These are not questions to answer quickly, but to reflect on, to look inside ourselves and perhaps, discover some uncomfortable but necessary truths.

Carl Jung already said it, "Until the unconscious becomes conscious, the subconscious will continue to run your life and you will call it destiny." So, let's make the unconscious conscious, shall we?

But don't worry, you are not alone in this journey. I am here with you, holding your hand every step of the way, reminding you that you are capable, that you are worthy of love and respect, and that you have the power to build the life you deserve.

You know, there is nothing wrong with wanting to be loved and appreciated. As humans, we long for connection, we long to be understood and accepted for who we are. But, as we have discussed in previous chapters, this desire becomes problematic when we depend on others for our emotional well-being, when we become dependent on their approval and affection in order to feel complete.

This is where emotional independence comes into play. As John Gottman wrote in "The Seven Principles for Making Marriage Work" (1999), "Emotional independence is the key to creating healthy relationships." When we are emotionally independent, we are not only able to take care of our own emotional needs, but we are also able to be present for others in an authentic and loving way.

But what does this look like in practice? How do we build healthy relationships from this place of emotional independence? Well, dear reader, this is where things get really interesting.

Building healthy relationships takes work, commitment and a lot of patience. But don't worry, you are not alone on this journey. I will be with you every step of the way, providing you with the tools, strategies and support you need to succeed.

The first step to building healthy relationships is to know your own needs and desires. What do you really want from your relationships? What do you need to feel loved, respected and supported? Remember, there are no right or wrong answers here, only what is true for you.

The second step is to communicate your needs and wants effectively. Remember what we talked about in Chapter 13 about assertiveness? The ability to express your needs without fear is crucial to building healthy relationships.

And finally, you must be able to set and maintain healthy boundaries. Boundaries are not walls that separate us from others, but signals that indicate how far others can go with us. Boundaries are an expression of our self-respect and self-respect, both for ourselves and for others.

But what do these principles look like in action? Well, that's what the next sections are for, where we will explore each of these aspects in more depth.

Let me tell you a story. Imagine Sandra. Sandra is a woman in her thirties, with a successful career and a wide circle of friends. But Sandra has an internal struggle; she often feels that she is not enough, that she has to try harder, do more, be more, to deserve love and acceptance. Her past relationships have been tumultuous, full of emotional ups and downs, and Sandra often feels trapped in a cycle of emotional dependency. Does this sound familiar? Have you ever felt what Sandra feels? Read on, my friend. Sandra's story may seem very familiar to you, but it can also be a source of inspiration and learning.

Sandra decided to take a step back and reflect on her past relationships. She realized that she often allowed the needs and desires of others to overshadow her own. She was so focused on making others happy that she forgot about her own happiness. So Sandra decided to make a change. She began to explore her own needs and desires, to understand what she really wanted from her relationships. Was it easy? Of course it wasn't. But Sandra knew it was a necessary step on her path to emotional independence.

Sandra also found that she had trouble communicating effectively. She often avoided conflict and kept her feelings to herself to keep the peace. But this only led to resentment and misunderstandings. So Sandra began practicing assertiveness. She began to express her needs and desires in a respectful but firm manner, and began to see positive changes in her relationships.

But the biggest change came when Sandra learned to set boundaries. She learned to say "no" when necessary, to protect her time and energy, to enforce her personal boundaries. It was a challenging, but also liberating process. Sandra realized that by setting boundaries, she was showing respect for herself and others.

And what happened to Sandra? Well, Sandra is still on her journey to emotional independence. She still has difficult days, days when she is tempted to fall into old patterns of dependency. But Sandra knows she's on the right path. She knows she is building healthier relationships, relationships that are based on mutual respect and self-love. And that, dear reader, is a big step toward emotional freedom.

But what about you, where are you on your journey? Are you ready to take the steps necessary to build healthier relationships? Are you ready to explore your own needs and desires, to communicate effectively, to set healthy boundaries? Remember, you don't have to do it alone. I am here to guide you, to support you, to help you discover your own path to emotional independence.

In the next section, we will delve even deeper into these topics. We'll talk about how you can use the tools and strategies we've learned to build healthy relationships and foster emotional independence. I'll show you how each piece fits into this complex puzzle of life, and together, we'll discover how it can help you break free from emotional dependence.

Setting healthy boundaries, practicing assertiveness, understanding your own needs and desires... these are not easy tasks, my friend. They require effort, dedication, and sometimes a little sweat and tears. But let me tell you, the rewards are worth it. It could be the difference between being trapped in a cycle of emotional dependency and finding true emotional freedom.

Think about it: What would your life be like if you were able to set healthy boundaries? How would your relationships change if you were able to communicate your needs and desires effectively? How would you feel if you were able to meet your own emotional needs, instead of relying on others to do so?

This is the promise of emotional independence, dear reader. It is not an easy road, but I promise you it is a road worth traveling.

And if you ever feel overwhelmed, remember: you are not alone. You have a fellow traveler in me, and together, we can face any challenge that comes our way. Remember Sandra's journey, remember the concepts we have explored in this chapter, and always remember that you have the power to change your life.

Are you ready to take the next step? Are you ready to dive deeper into the waters of emotional independence and discover what awaits you in Chapter 20, "Emotional Independence in Relationships"? I promise you it will be an enriching and eye-opening exploration, one that can transform your life and your relationships in ways you can only begin to imagine.

Come with me, my friend. Let us continue our journey. The depths of emotional independence await us.

Chapter 20: Emotional Independence in Couples Relationships

We have traveled a long and twisted road together, haven't we, my friend? We have explored the roots of emotional dependency, unmasked its disguises, unraveled its subtle symbols and understood the crucial role of self-esteem in its maintenance. We have learned to set boundaries, to be assertive, to practice self-care, to bust myths and forge new beliefs. But now, we come to new territory, territory that often feels as complicated as it is mysterious: relationships.

Why talk about relationships, you ask? Well, relationships are the main stage where emotional dependency plays out. They are like a mirror, reflecting our self-esteem, our insecurities, our strengths and our weaknesses. And, of course, they can also be a powerful catalyst for personal growth and emotional independence.

Remember when we talked about healthy relationships in Chapter 19? There we pointed out that healthy relationships are not only possible, they are the key to our emotional well-being. But now, let's dig deeper. We're going to explore how we can foster emotional independence in our relationships. Are you ready? Take a deep breath, because we're about to embark on one of the most important stages of our journey.

Throughout our lives, we experience different types of love: platonic love, familial love, romantic love. However, in no other relationship do our fears, hopes, desires and behavioral patterns manifest themselves as much as in couple relationships. For many people, these relationships become a cycle of dependency and struggle for control. But it doesn't have to be that way. We can learn to love without losing our emotional independence, and that, my dear reader, is our goal in this chapter.

Imagine for a moment a relationship in which you feel valued, appreciated, and respected. A relationship in which you can express your needs and desires without fear of being judged or rejected. A relationship in which you feel free to be yourself, without fear of losing the other person. Sounds good, doesn't it? And I assure you, it's not just a fantasy. This kind of relationship is possible, and I'll show you how you can achieve it.

But what exactly does emotional independence mean in relationships? What does it look like? How does it feel? And most importantly, how can we foster it? Well, to answer these questions, we first need to understand what emotional independence means. So, let's do a little recap.

Emotional independence does not mean that you should be an emotional hermit, disconnected from others. No, quite the opposite. As we saw in Chapter 10, emotional independence means having the ability to meet your own emotional needs, without depending on others for your well-being and happiness. It is having a healthy sense of autonomy and self-esteem, and having the ability to set healthy boundaries.

Now, going back to couple relationships, emotional independence is essentially the ability to maintain your autonomy within the relationship. It is the balance between the "I" and the "we". As the famous psychologist and author Harville Hendrix says in his book "Getting the Love You

Want" (1988), "a healthy couple relationship is one in which each individual maintains his or her identity while being in touch with the identity of the other."

And how do we achieve this? Well, as with any skill, it takes practice and patience. But here are some tips to help you on your way.

First, it is important that you know yourself. Remember what we discussed in Chapter 8 about the importance of understanding our own emotions. Only when you know yourself can you know what you need and want in a relationship. Therefore, take some time to reflect on your needs, desires, values, and goals.

Second, learn to set boundaries. As we discussed in Chapter 22, boundaries are essential to maintaining our autonomy and emotional well-being. Make sure your partner respects your boundaries and vice versa.

Third, practice open and honest communication. While it may be uncomfortable or difficult at first, sharing your thoughts, feelings and concerns with your partner can strengthen your relationship and help you maintain your emotional independence. As noted psychologist and author Susan Forward mentions in her work "Emotional Blackmail: When the People in Your Life Use Fear, Obligation, and Guilt to Manipulate You" (1997), effective communication is the cornerstone of healthy, autonomous relationships.

Finally, don't forget to take care of yourself. Self-compassion and self-care are fundamental to emotional independence. So make sure you take time for yourself, to do things you enjoy and that make you feel good.

Now, I'm talking to you about all this because I know it's possible. Remember when I mentioned that relationships can be a powerful catalyst for personal growth? Well, this is a case in point. Through our relationships, we can learn to love and be loved in a healthy way, without losing our emotional independence.

But I also want you to know that this road is not easy. There will be moments of doubt, of fear, of confusion. But you are not alone. I am here with you, walking beside you, and together we will make it. Because remember, my dear friend, emotional independence is not a destination, but a journey. A journey of self-knowledge, self-care, and self-love. And I promise you, it's worth every step. Will you join me on the next one?

Well, now that we've covered the basics and touched on the essentials of emotional independence in relationships, it's time to dive deeper. It's time to talk about how you can put all of this into practice, will you join me?

Let's explore a case study. Imagine you have a relationship with a wonderful person who, in many ways, is a perfect match for you. But there is one issue that always brings you into conflict. This topic can be anything from opinions on politics to how often you want to leave the house.

When this issue comes up, you feel that your partner does not respect your point of view. You try to express yourself, to set your boundaries, but it seems to you that everything is in vain. Your partner just doesn't seem to understand. You start to question yourself, your emotions, your needs. You begin to feel that you are losing your emotional independence.

So, what do you do? Do you break up with the person you love just because of a problem? Or do you resign yourself and sacrifice your emotional well-being to keep the peace?

That's where emotional independence comes in. Psychologist and author Daniel Goleman, in his book "Emotional Intelligence" (1995), stresses that the ability to manage our own emotions and those of others is crucial to our well-being and success in life. Specifically, in situations like this, emotional independence provides you with the necessary tools to manage this conflict in a healthy way.

The first step, as always, is to acknowledge your emotions. Admit your feelings of frustration, sadness, anger. It is normal to have these emotions. They are a sign that something is not right. Acknowledge them and accept them.

Then try to understand what is really bothering you. Is it the lack of respect for your point of view? Is it the feeling of not being listened to? Or is it something deeper, perhaps related to your self-esteem or your need for approval?

Once you understand what the real problem is, you can begin to take steps to solve it. Talk to your partner. Express your feelings and needs clearly and assertively. Remember, your emotions are valid. Your needs are important. And you deserve to be heard.

Last but not least, keep in mind that sometimes it may be necessary to seek professional help. A psychotherapist or counselor can provide you with valuable tools to manage conflict and maintain your emotional independence.

I know this may seem overwhelming. But remember, every step you take, every challenge you overcome, brings you closer to your goal of emotional independence. And I'm here with you, every step of the way.

Now, are you ready to go ahead and learn more about how to maintain your emotional independence? Because, believe me, there's a lot more to discover. And I can't wait to share it with you. So take a breath, get your strength back, and let's keep moving forward together. Because remember, this journey is just beginning. Will you join me?

Well, we've come a long and fruitful way in this chapter, don't you think? From discussing what emotional independence entails in couple relationships, to exploring the challenges that can arise and how to deal with them. And yet, this is only one chapter in our great adventure, and there are many more to go.

We've talked about how to recognize your own emotions, how to communicate them effectively, and how to handle conflict in a way that respects both your needs and those of your partner. All of this is crucial to maintaining your emotional independence in a relationship. But you know what else is important? Knowing that you are on a journey, that each step, each challenge, brings you closer to your goal.

Along this journey, you may encounter obstacles. You may stumble, you may fall. But remember, that doesn't mean you've failed. It means you're learning. And every time you get up, every time you overcome a challenge, you'll be stronger, more resilient and closer to your goal.

And we are here, with you, every step of the way. We are here to guide you, to support you and to celebrate your victories. Because even though this is your journey, you don't have to do it alone. We're here with you, and together, we're going to get you where you want to go.

Now, what's next? Well, now that we've talked about how to maintain your emotional independence in relationships, the next chapter will take you to a new level of self-knowledge and personal growth. We're going to talk about personal freedom and growth: continuous development. You will learn how emotional freedom is not a destination, but a constant process of growth and evolution.

Are you ready to move forward, to keep growing, to keep moving towards the emotional freedom you deserve? Are you ready to embark on the next chapter of your journey? Because I'm eager to keep sharing this journey with you. And I can't wait to see what the next chapter has in store for you.

But remember, this is just the beginning. And every step you take, every challenge you overcome, is one step closer to your goal. And believe me, the road ahead is exciting. So, will you join me for the next chapter? I promise, you won't want to miss it. So take a breather, get your strength back, and let's get going. Together.

Chapter 21: Freedom and Personal Growth: Continuous Development

Today I would like to talk to you about a journey, but not just any journey, but one that we all take, a journey that never ends. It is about our personal journey of growth and development. It is important, don't you think? Life is a constant learning and evolution, and emotional freedom is no exception to this principle.

Consider this: personal growth is like climbing a mountain. Each step takes you closer to the top, but even when you reach the top, there is always a new mountain to climb. The summit you reached simply gives you a new perspective, a broader view. Emotional freedom is similar; it is not a fixed destination, but a path that continually unfolds before us, a path that always offers us more to learn and explore.

So why is this important to understand? Well, by understanding that personal growth and emotional freedom are ongoing processes, you free yourself from the pressure of having to "get" somewhere. You free yourself from the urge to be "perfect." You understand that every step you take on your journey, every achievement, every mistake, every lesson learned, is valuable in itself.

Have you ever stopped to reflect on how you have grown and changed over the years? Have you noticed how your emotions, your relationships, your beliefs, your skills and your goals have evolved? This is personal growth. It is a continuous change, a series of transformations that lead us to become more authentic and emotionally free versions of ourselves.

But what exactly does personal growth mean? According to Mihaly Csikszentmihalyi, psychologist and author of "Flow: A Psychology of Happiness" (1990), personal growth involves expanding our awareness and improving our abilities to handle life's challenges. It is a process of self-discovery and self-improvement. It is the art of becoming the best version of oneself.

So, are you ready to embark on this journey of personal growth and emotional freedom? Are you ready to explore the heights and depths of your own being, to discover who you really are and what you really want out of life? Because, if you are ready, I promise you that this journey will be one of the most exciting and rewarding adventures of your life.

Go ahead, start climbing that mountain. Every step is a step toward greater emotional freedom. Every step is a step toward greater authenticity and personal fulfillment. And remember, you are not alone on this journey. We are here, with you, every step of the way. So, ready for the next step in your journey of personal growth and emotional freedom? I look forward to seeing you in the next section of this chapter.

Now that you are on the road to personal growth and emotional freedom, I would like to talk to you about a couple of concepts that you may find useful. In his book "The 7 Habits of Highly Effective People" (1989), Stephen Covey talks about "proactivity" and "responsibility". According to Covey, proactivity is the ability to control our responses to circumstances, rather than allowing circumstances to control us. Meanwhile, responsibility is the ability to take ownership of our lives, our actions, and our decisions.

Think about it, how many times have you allowed external circumstances or other people's emotions to determine your emotional state? How many times have you relinquished control of your emotions to other people or situations? This is a common pattern, especially in people with emotional dependency. But, here comes the good news: you have the ability to change this pattern. You have the ability to be proactive and take responsibility for your emotions.

You may be wondering, how can I do that? Well, this is where personal growth plays a crucial role. Through self-awareness and the development of emotional skills, you can learn to respond in a healthier way to situations and emotions. You can learn to set boundaries, say "no" when necessary, express your needs and desires effectively, and manage your emotions in a healthier way.

This is where another important figure in the field of psychology comes into play, Carl Rogers, who in his book "The Process of Becoming a Person" (1961), talks about the concept of "self-acceptance". According to Rogers, self-acceptance is a crucial step towards personal growth. It consists of recognizing and accepting our emotions, thoughts and behaviors, even those we consider "negative" or "undesirable." By accepting these parts of ourselves, we can begin to understand and eventually change them.

See how it all connects? Proactivity, responsibility, self-acceptance... all these concepts are fundamental pieces of the puzzle of personal growth and emotional freedom. And here comes the most exciting part: you have the power to put these pieces together. You have the power to embark on this exciting journey of self-discovery and transformation. So, are you ready to take the next step on this journey? Are you ready to explore these concepts further and discover how you can apply them in your life? I look forward to seeing you in the next section, where we will delve deeper into these topics and I will provide you with some practical tools to help you on your journey.

Have you ever wondered why some trees grow taller and sturdier than others? If you think about it, the answer is simple. It all comes down to their roots and the soil in which they are planted. Trees with strong, well-nourished roots are able to withstand the strongest storms, stand up in tough times and reach impressive heights. In a way, we human beings are like trees. Our growth and development also depend on our inner "roots," that is, our emotional, mental and spiritual abilities.

Let's talk about a concrete example to illustrate these concepts. Imagine a person named Luis. Luis has suffered from emotional dependency for many years, but he has finally decided to make a change. He has started reading self-help books, going to therapy and participating in support groups. He is working hard to improve his self-esteem and learn to set boundaries. In other words, Luis is cultivating his inner "roots".

And you know what? As Luis grows stronger internally, he also begins to notice external changes. He feels more confident, is able to express his needs and desires more effectively, and no longer allows other people's emotions or actions to determine his mood. Like a tree with strong roots, Luis is growing and flourishing.

Luis' story is just one example, but I hope it helps you understand the importance of personal growth on the road to emotional freedom. As Abraham Maslow mentions in his work "Motivation and Personality" (1954), each of us has the potential for growth and self-transcendence. We all have the capacity to overcome our limitations and reach our highest aspirations.

And what does this mean for you? It means that, no matter how hard your struggle with emotional dependency has been, you too have the potential for growth and transformation. You too can strengthen your inner "roots" and become the person you have always wanted to be.

Are you excited, feeling that tingle of anticipation? Well, my dear reader, this is just the beginning. In the next section, I will provide you with more tools and strategies to help you foster your personal growth and move forward on your path to emotional freedom. Are you ready to continue this adventure? Here we go!

Remember when I told you about Luis, who decided to take control of his life, face his emotional dependency and take important steps to cultivate his inner "roots"? Well, I want you to imagine yourself in Luis' place. But before you feel overwhelmed, let me remind you that you are not alone in this struggle. I am here with you, walking every step with you, and I know you are stronger than you think. But you know what's exciting? The fact that you're about to find out for yourself!

Think of all the great thinkers and writers who have left their mark on history. Many of them, like Viktor Frankl in "Man's Search for Meaning" (1946), have highlighted the importance of facing and overcoming our inner struggles in order to achieve meaningful personal growth and development. This is exactly what you are doing right now. You are on the path to authentic personal transformation, and I am honored to witness it.

Now, what can we expect on this last part of our journey? This is where it gets even more exciting. In the next section, we're going to put into practice everything we've learned so far. We're going to explore new ways to apply these concepts to your daily life, and to further strengthen your inner "roots". Most importantly, we will celebrate your accomplishments and appreciate each step you have taken on this path to emotional independence.

My dear friend, you are about to enter uncharted territory, full of challenges as well as rewards. You may ask yourself, am I ready for this? Let me answer with a resounding, "Yes, you are! You are ready to grow and flourish, to discover your true capabilities and to break free from the chains of emotional dependency. Doesn't that sound exciting?

So, what do you say we dive into the next chapter together? In it, we will explore the importance of setting boundaries in interpersonal relationships, an essential skill to maintain and protect your new emotional freedom. Are you ready to continue this exciting adventure? I promise it will be a transformational experience! Now, take a deep breath, smile and let me take you by the hand on this next phase of your journey to emotional freedom. Here we go!

Chapter 22: The Importance of Boundaries in Interpersonal Relationships

You have come this far, following a path of self-knowledge and self-affirmation, and with it you have begun to see that emotional independence is not an unattainable goal, but a reality that you can cultivate day by day. Isn't it wonderful how our journey together is giving you the tools to be the best version of yourself?

Now that we've talked about how to free yourself from emotional dependence and how to cultivate emotional independence, it's time to dive into a crucial topic for maintaining that independence: boundaries in interpersonal relationships. Why do you think it's important to talk about boundaries in relationships? What are these boundaries really and why are they so essential?

Boundaries are like the fences that protect a garden, or the walls that define a room. They are the invisible barriers we set up to protect our emotional well-being and our personal space. Boundaries allow us to have control over our own lives, protect our needs and prevent others from manipulating us or taking us for granted. When we set clear boundaries, we are communicating to others what our personal and emotional space is, what we are willing to accept and what we are not.

Having healthy boundaries is essential to our relationships because it allows us to maintain our autonomy while interacting with others. In other words, it allows us to love and be loved without sacrificing our emotional well-being.

Can you imagine how liberating it can be to have this kind of control over your relationships? Imagine for a moment that you are like a country with clear and defined borders. These borders protect you from invasion and conflict. But at the same time, they allow you to have peaceful and healthy relationships with other countries. In the same way, boundaries in your relationships protect you and allow you to interact in healthy ways with others.

But why are boundaries so important to maintaining emotional independence? Well, as I mentioned in Chapter 20, a crucial part of emotional independence is the ability to maintain healthy relationships without becoming dependent. Boundaries help you achieve just that. By setting clear boundaries, you are ensuring that you can love and be loved without sacrificing your autonomy.

In addition, boundaries are also a way to practice self-care. Remember, in Chapter 9 we talked about the importance of self-care in the release process. Well, boundaries are a way to protect your emotional and mental well-being. When you set clear boundaries, you are saying "I value and respect myself enough to protect my personal and emotional space."

So, now that we understand how valuable boundaries are, how do we set them? How can we communicate our needs to others in a way that is respectful but firm? Those are the issues we will explore in detail in the following sections.

So, my friend, as we move into this new territory, I want you to join me with an open mind and a willingness to learn. In this part, we will begin to explore the art of setting healthy boundaries in our relationships.

Nina Brown, in her book "Boundaries: A Guide for Teens" (2011), reminds us that boundaries are not walls, but rather bridges that allow us to connect with others in a healthy and respectful way. And, like bridges, boundaries require constant maintenance and care to function properly. Have you ever thought of your personal boundaries as bridges that connect you to others?

You can begin to set healthy boundaries by first identifying your emotional and physical needs. This involves a good deal of self-knowledge, which brings us back to the concepts we explored in the previous chapters on self-assertion and self-understanding. Recall Eleanor Roosevelt with her famous line, "No one can make you feel inferior without your consent." In this sense, no one can invade your boundaries without your permission. The first step in setting boundaries is, therefore, to understand what you need and want in your relationships.

But what happens when someone crosses a boundary you've set? This is where communication comes into play. You will need to learn to express your needs and feelings clearly and respectfully. In Chapter 13, we discussed assertiveness as a key skill for expressing your needs without fear. Remember when we talked about the importance of expressing your needs in an assertive, non-aggressive way?

Here, I must emphasize the importance of practicing assertiveness in setting and enforcing your boundaries. It is critical to learn how to communicate effectively, without being aggressive or passive. As psychologist Albert Ellis noted in his book "How To Be Your Own Best Friend" (1971), assertiveness involves "standing up for your personal rights, expressing your thoughts, feelings and beliefs directly, honestly and appropriately, without violating the rights of others." Essentially, assertiveness is the key to maintaining your boundaries without damaging your relationships.

Do you find it challenging? Don't worry, you're in the right place at the right time to learn. So, take a deep breath and get ready to dive into the practice of boundary setting, which is an essential element of your emotional independence. Are you ready to continue this important chapter of your journey to emotional freedom? Remember, you're here because you care, and that's already a big step. So let's keep moving forward, always together, always growing.

Now, you are ready to delve deeper into how to establish and maintain those boundaries that will protect your emotional well-being. Like a careful gardener who establishes fences to protect his precious crops, you too are working to protect the preciousness of your emotional self.

Personal development expert Brene Brown, author of "The Gifts of Imperfection" (2010), talks about the importance of setting boundaries as a way to honor our own dignity and respect the dignity of others. In her words, "Dignity is not based on what we can offer others, but on how we value and respect ourselves." Don't you find it fascinating how boundaries can be an affirmation of our worth and an invitation to others to respect us?

Also, it's important to remember that your boundaries are yours and no one else's. You may have a friend or loved one who is perfectly comfortable with a certain degree of physical contact or intimate conversations. You may have a friend or loved one who is perfectly comfortable with a certain degree of physical contact or intimate conversations, while you may find it uncomfortable. And you know what? That's perfectly fine. There is no universal manual that defines what your personal boundaries should be. It is you who has the right and responsibility to define them.

Now, let's do an exercise together. Imagine that you are in a situation where you feel that your boundary has been violated. Maybe someone made a thoughtless comment about your appearance, or maybe you feel burned out from constantly helping a friend without getting anything in return. How do you feel in that situation? Can you identify which boundary was crossed? Now, imagine how you could handle that situation differently, using assertive communication to set your boundaries. What would that look like?

Don't forget that it is completely natural and necessary to adjust your boundaries as you change and grow. As mentioned in "Boundaries: When to Say Yes, How to Say No to Take Control of Your Life" by Cloud and Townsend (1992), your boundaries are a living part of you, and as such, they should be able to change and adapt as you do.

I hope this makes you feel more equipped and empowered to begin the task of setting and enforcing your own boundaries. But let's not stop here. Let's continue to go deeper into this journey of self-discovery and empowerment. Are you ready to move forward, my brave fellow traveler?

Now, here we are, at the end of our deep dive into the ocean of personal boundaries. You have gained a clearer understanding of what they are, why they are important and how they can be a safe haven for your self-esteem and personal identity. You've also learned that boundaries are unique to each individual and that it's up to you to set your own in a way that aligns with your personal needs and values. Most importantly, you have gained the tools and strategies to respectfully and assertively enforce your boundaries.

It is fascinating how in our journey together we have seen that boundaries are not barriers that isolate us, but rather are bridges that allow us to interact with others in a healthy and respectful way. And remember the words of Harriet Lerner in "The Dance of Anger" (1985), "The installation of clear boundaries is the key to preserving self-esteem, your time and energy, and your emotional well-being."

I want you to take a moment to appreciate how far you have come. You have shown incredible courage and determination every step of the way. And while it may not always be easy, every small victory, every new discovery about yourself, every breakthrough, no matter how small, is a sign of your growth and strength.

And now, how about a little preview of what's in store for you in the next chapter? In it, I'll take you by the hand to explore the powerful and encouraging world of personal transformation. We will discover together how people who have been in your shoes, who have dealt with emotional dependency, have managed to do a 180-degree turnaround and become emotionally autonomous and self-confident beings. I assure you that their stories of success and overcoming will inspire you and give you a renewed sense of hope and confidence in your own path to emotional freedom.

So, what do you think, are you ready to open the next chapter of this exciting journey? As always, I'll be here with you, every step of the way, guiding you, supporting you and celebrating with you every new discovery and breakthrough you make. Let's go for it!

Chapter 23: From Dependent to Self-Employed: Success and Overcoming Stories

Dear reader, have you ever heard the phrase "success leaves clues"? This concept, popularized by Tony Robbins in "Awakening the Giant Within" (1991), suggests that by studying and understanding other people's success stories, we can learn valuable lessons that will help us on our own journey. So what better way to inspire and motivate you on your journey to emotional independence than by listening to stories of people who have already been where you are now and who have succeeded in making the momentous journey from emotional dependence to autonomy?

These stories are important, my reader, because each of them is a living testimony that personal transformation is possible and achievable. Moreover, these narratives of self-improvement and achievement allow us to explore and understand how the various tools and strategies we have discussed thus far apply in real-life situations and contexts. They provide concrete, palpable insight into the benefits of emotional autonomy and freedom from emotional dependency. But what makes these stories so powerful and motivating? Well, the answer lies in our own biology and how our brain processes narratives and stories.

You see, when we listen to or read a story, our brain doesn't just passively register the information, it actively engages, imagining itself in the situations described. A 2006 study, published in the journal NeuroImage by Gregory Berns' team of neuroscientists, showed that listening to a story can elicit a real emotional response in our brain, and these emotional responses can be very powerful for learning and change.

These answers are what will help you integrate and apply the lessons from these success stories to your own path to emotional independence. They will allow you to explore how the tools and strategies we have discussed so far can be applied in different contexts and real-life situations.

But what would you say if I told you that these stories of self-improvement don't only come from celebrities or notable individuals? Actually, the most powerful ones tend to come from ordinary people, just like you and me. People who have struggled with emotional dependency and found their way to autonomy.

Some of these stories come from people who have gone through great adversity, while others are more discreet, but no less valuable. Each carries with it a message of hope, resilience and self-transformation.

But wait, don't you think we've been talking for a while now, you and I? Don't you think it would be wonderful to know first hand these stories of overcoming and success? So, get your cup of coffee ready, settle into your favorite chair, because in the next few segments, I'm going to introduce you to some of these extraordinary people and their inspiring stories.

Fernando's story is one of emotional overcoming of a toxic relationship. He lived in a constant state of anxiety and insecurity, hooked to a person who gave him nothing but pain and stress. But what exactly happened? How did Fernando go from living under the shadow of another person to being an autonomous, emotionally independent individual?

Fernando recalls that the turning point came when he read a quote from psychologist and writer Susan Forward, in her book "Emotional Blackmail" (1997). The passage read, "The key to emotional freedom lies in discovering our own inner strength and realizing that we are in control of our own lives." This phrase resonated with Fernando. He began to question his situation and reflect on his own decisions.

She decided it was time to get help. He joined a local support group and began working with a therapist who specialized in emotional dependency. He began to better understand his situation and learn how to break the cycle of dependency he was trapped in.

Fernando worked hard to change his life. He learned to set boundaries, improve his self-esteem and rebuild his identity. Every step he took, every small victory, every moment of self-understanding and self-love, was one more brick in the construction of his new life.

Today, Fernando is a new man. He has regained his confidence and lives his life autonomously, aware of his emotions and needs. He has discovered that he can have healthy and satisfying relationships without losing his identity in the process. In his words, "I have learned that I don't need to depend on anyone to be happy. I now know that true happiness comes from within, from loving and respecting yourself."

Don't you think it's an incredible journey? And that's not all, there are many more stories like Fernando's that can serve as inspiration and hope. I assure you that, with dedication and the right tools, you too can become the protagonist of an overcoming story. Are you ready to continue this journey?

Indeed, stories of overcoming, like Fernando's, are a living demonstration that it is possible to break the chains of emotional dependency and transform oneself into an autonomous and emotionally healthy individual. They are not just words in a book or abstract theories. They are real people, with real stories, with real battles that have been won.

As psychologist Judith S. Beck mentioned in her book "Cognitive Behavior Therapy: Basics and Beyond" (1995), "Lasting change requires constant and committed work". Fernando, Ana, and many others, are living examples of this truth. They did that constant and committed work, and as a result, they succeeded in transforming their lives.

Of course, every overcoming story is unique. Each person has his or her own challenges, his or her own patterns of thinking and behavior, his or her own experiences. However, there is one thing in common in all of these stories: the decision to change and the willingness to work to achieve it.

We have reached the end of this chapter, but not the end of the journey. We have explored together the paths taken by those who have conquered emotional dependence and transformed themselves into autonomous beings. I hope these stories inspire you, give you hope and make you see that, with effort and dedication, you too can be the protagonist of your own story of overcoming.

In the next chapter, we're going to explore the strategies you can use to maintain your emotional independence once you've achieved it. It's a bumpy road, but don't worry, I'll be here to help you get over each one. Are you ready for the next step on this journey to emotional freedom? I assure you that each page will bring you a little closer to your goal. Shall we go together?

Chapter 24: Maintaining Emotional Independence: Strategies for Avoiding Relapse

Maintaining emotional independence is like tending a garden. Have you ever had the opportunity to grow one? If so, you probably know that after you plant the seeds and watch the first plants sprout, the work doesn't end there. In fact, that's when the work really begins. Every day you must water those little plants, pull weeds that threaten to choke them, protect them from inclement weather and pests. In short, you must care for them with care so that they can flourish and bear fruit. Emotional independence is like that garden, and you are its gardener.

You have come a long way on this journey. You have learned to recognize the signs of emotional dependency, you have explored its origin and its impact on your life, you have identified the patterns of thought and behavior that kept you bound, and you have worked to change them. You have learned to value yourself, to respect yourself, to take care of yourself. You have learned to set boundaries, to express your needs, and to build healthy relationships. All of this has taken a great deal of effort, and you can certainly be proud of what you have accomplished.

However, it is crucial that you understand that, just as the gardener must continue to care for his plants even after they have bloomed, you must continue to care for your emotional independence even after you have achieved it. So, in this chapter, we will explore strategies you can use to maintain that independence and avoid relapse.

Imagine you are in a forest and you realize that you have strayed off the path. What would you do? You would probably look for signs to help you get back on the right path. The same is true on our journey to emotional independence. Even if you have come a long way, there is always the risk of getting sidetracked, of returning to the old patterns of thinking and behavior that kept you tied to emotional dependency. That's why you need to be clear about the signs that you are drifting and what you can do to get back on track.

Remember when we talked about the subtle symbols of dependency in Chapter 5? Let's revisit that topic, but this time, from a different perspective. Instead of looking for signs of dependence, let's look for signs of independence. How can you tell if you are maintaining your emotional independence? What are the signs that tell you that you are on the right path? And what can you do when you stray?

Think about it for a moment. What do you think are the signs of emotional independence? What changes have you noticed in yourself since you started this journey? Remember, this is not a test. There are no right or wrong answers. It is simply an invitation to reflect on your own process of change.

How would it be if I told you that you are not alone in this process? That there are a number of guides you can rely on, written by great authors who have researched and lived through these processes. As Pema Chödrön would say, in her acclaimed work "When Things Fall Apart" (1997), "Nothing goes away until it has taught us what we need to learn". These words hold a great truth, and that is that every experience, no matter how hard it is, always brings with it a lesson to be learned.

Emotional dependence, that old path we used to walk, was a familiar, albeit painful, path. But now, on this new path of emotional independence, we may feel lost, insecure. This is normal. As Brené Brown stated in her book "The Gifts of Imperfection" (2010), leaving our comfort zone is always a challenge, but it is also an opportunity to grow, to learn, to develop as individuals.

So what can we do when we stray from the path of emotional independence? Well, the first step is to recognize that we have strayed. This is not easy. Sometimes, we can slip into denial, we can think that everything is okay when it's really not. But, as Carl Jung pointed out, what we resist, persists. If we resist the idea that we have gone astray, if we refuse to see reality as it is, we will only make the problem persist. Therefore, the first step is to recognize that we have strayed.

Next, we can seek support. Perhaps from a trusted friend, a family member, a therapist. As John Bowlby pointed out in his attachment theory, we all need a safe harbor, someone to offer us support and security in times of crisis. That doesn't mean we are dependent. It simply means that we are human and, as such, we need emotional connections.

Finally, we can use the tools we have learned on our journey to emotional independence. We may need to reinforce our boundaries, we may need to practice more self-affirmation, we may need to reconnect with our emotions. Remember, each of us is unique and what works for one may not work for another. So, listen to your intuition, your inner wisdom. It will guide you to what you need at any given moment.

I encourage you to reflect on this. Have you ever experienced a relapse in your process towards emotional independence? How did you realize that you had strayed? What did you do to get back on the right path? What did you learn from that experience? As the great poet Rumi would say, "the wound is the place where the light enters". So, don't be afraid to look at your wounds. They will show you the way to the light, to your true self.

Let's look at a concrete example that will clearly illustrate what we have been discussing. Imagine someone, let's call him Juan, who has spent most of his life in emotionally dependent relationships. One day, after reading a life-changing book (perhaps this very one you are holding in your hands), he decides that the time has come to change. He feels motivated, full of hope. He begins to practice self-care, self-affirmation, to set limits. Little by little, you begin to feel that you are getting your life back.

But one day, she runs into an old partner, the person with whom she shared so many moments, good and bad. And without realizing it, he falls back into old patterns of emotional dependency. He feels lost, disappointed with himself, has all his progress been in vain?

At this point, Juan has two options. He could indulge in self-criticism, in a sense of failure. Or he could remember the words of the great Maya Angelou, in her poem "Still I Rise" (1978): "You may beat me with your words, you may cut me with your eyes, you may kill me with your hate, but still, like the air, I will rise".

Juan decides to choose the second option. He recognizes that he has relapsed, but instead of punishing himself for it, he decides to learn from the experience. He seeks support from his loved ones and his therapist. He reviews the tools he learned on his path to emotional independence and realizes that he needs to work more on his emotional boundaries.

Through this experience, Juan learns a valuable lesson. He learns that the road to emotional independence is not a straight path, but a road full of curves and detours. He learns that relapses are a natural part of the process and that, far from being a sign of failure, they are an opportunity to learn and grow. Learn that, as the famous psychologist Carl Rogers said, "a well-functioning person implies an ongoing process of change".

So, my friend, if you ever find yourself in Juan's situation, remember: relapses are part of the process. They are not a failure, they are an opportunity to learn. And you can always, always get back on track. Because, as the great poet Robert Frost said, "Two roads forked in a forest and I...I took the one less traveled by. And that has made all the difference.

Ah, and there you have it. You've reached the last section of this chapter and I'd like to remind you of something you know, but may need to hear right now: Your path to emotional independence is valuable, and so are you. But what does that really mean? It means that every experience you have on this path, even relapses, are learning opportunities.

As mentioned earlier, relapses are a natural part of the change process. But how can they be useful? Well, they provide you with a valuable opportunity to learn more about yourself and your triggers. They also give you a chance to put the tools you've learned into practice and strengthen your resilience.

Throughout this chapter, we have explored the nature of relapses and discussed various strategies for managing them, including maintaining a learning attitude, seeking support, and reevaluating your coping strategies. Recall the words of Albert Ellis, the famous psychotherapist and pioneer of cognitive-behavioral therapy, in his book Overcoming Destructive Beliefs, Feelings, and Behaviors: New Directions for Rational Emotive Behavior Therapy (2001), who said, "The best way to get over something is to learn from it."

So if you ever find yourself relapsing, remember: You are not alone. You have not failed. You are on a path of learning and growth. And every step on that path, every challenge overcome, every relapse overcome, takes you one step closer to your goal of emotional independence.

My dear friend, we are about to embark on the last chapter of this journey together. The next chapter, "Emotional Dependence and the Hope of Change: A Healthy, Autonomous Future," is full of inspiration and practical strategies to keep you on the path to emotional independence. We'll delve into the territory of hope and explore how you can continue to build a healthy, autonomous future, even in the midst of challenges. Are you ready to take the next step? I promise you, it will be worth it. So, when you're ready, turn the page and let's continue this journey together.

Chapter 25: Emotional Dependence and the Hope for Change: A Healthy and Autonomous Future

Have you ever watched the sunrise, felt the freshness of the morning breeze, seen the first light of day paint the sky in vibrant colors and witnessed the sun slowly rise, bringing with it a new day, a new opportunity? If you have, then you intuitively understand a truth that nature teaches us every day: there is always room for a new beginning.

But what does this really mean for you, here and now, at the end of the journey you have made through the pages of this book? Let me suggest a possibility. It means that, whatever path you have traveled so far, whatever degree of emotional dependency you have experienced, you always have the option to change. You can always choose a new beginning, you can always opt for hope. It is not easy, of course, but it is possible. And that, my dear reader, is a powerful thing.

Let's begin this chapter by asking ourselves, what is hope? According to psychologist Charles R. Snyder, author of "The Psychology of Hope: You Can Get There from Here" (1994), hope is a motivating force, an engine that propels us forward, allowing us to imagine a better future and giving us the energy to work toward it. Hope, says Snyder, is composed of two elements: the "way" and the "will". The "pathway" refers to our ability to chart a path toward our goals, to imagine and plan how to achieve them. The "will," on the other hand, refers to our determination to follow that path, to overcome the obstacles that stand in our way.

Can you see how this applies to your path to emotional independence? You have the "way," in the form of the tools and strategies we have explored throughout this book. You have the "will," as evidenced by your commitment to read to this point and your desire to overcome emotional dependence. But there is something else that hope can offer you on this path, something we often overlook: the ability to dream, to imagine a different future, to envision an autonomous and healthy "self."

And no, I'm not talking about daydreaming or building castles in the air. I'm talking about a kind of visualization based on reality, on your true capabilities and potential. Remember Chapter 10, where we discussed the importance of self-affirmation and identity reconstruction? This is a good time to remember those lessons.

What kind of person do you want to be? How do you see yourself in your relationships, in your work, in your hobbies? How do you see yourself managing your emotions, your needs, your limits? Don't limit yourself. Imagine the best version of yourself. Visualize a future where you are autonomous, healthy, satisfied and emotionally balanced. And not only that, imagine a future where you can contribute positively to the lives of others from your autonomy.

You may ask yourself, can this type of visualization really help me overcome emotional dependence? Not only I assure you, but also several scientific studies support this claim. A notable example is the work of psychologist Martin Seligman, one of the fathers of positive psychology, who in his book "Flourish: A Visionary New Understanding of Happiness and

Well-being" (2011), highlights the power of positive visualization to motivate significant changes in our lives.

This concept is also supported by Ellen Langer, a social psychologist at Harvard University, who in "Mindfulness" (1989), emphasizes the importance of mindfulness and the ability to imagine new possibilities to create positive changes in our lives.

However, it is important to emphasize that visualization does not work like a magic wand. It is not enough to imagine a better future, you have to actively work to make it a reality. And this is where other skills that we have explored in this book come into play, such as assertiveness, self-assertion, self-care and the creation of support networks. These are the tools with which you will build that future you are envisioning.

It might interest you to know that there is a metaphor often used in cognitive therapy to illustrate this process: that of the garden. Imagine for a moment that your mind is a garden. In this garden, emotional dependency is like an invasive plant that has grown out of control, choking out the other plants and upsetting the balance of the ecosystem. The work of freeing yourself from emotional dependency is similar to that of a gardener who must pull up these invasive plants. But pulling up the invasive plant is not enough, you must also plant new seeds, seeds of emotional autonomy, of self-esteem, of communication skills, and you must take care of them so that they can grow and flourish.

This requires work, patience and perseverance. It will not happen overnight, but each small step you take, each seed you plant, will bring you a little closer to that garden of autonomy and emotional health that you are envisioning. So I invite you to keep working on yourself, to keep cultivating yourself, to keep taking care of yourself. Remember, you are like that dawn I mentioned at the beginning: there is always room for a new beginning, there is always hope.

Remember when we talked about boundaries in interpersonal relationships in chapter 22? These boundaries are like fences that protect our mental garden. Healthy boundaries help us keep invasive plants at bay and provide the space needed for our plants of self-esteem, autonomy, and communication skills to grow and thrive.

You may be asking yourself right now: How can I set healthy boundaries? How can I protect my mental garden without isolating myself from the world? These are crucial questions, and although we have already discussed some answers in previous chapters, let me highlight a few key points.

First, it is important to remember that setting boundaries does not mean closing yourself off from interpersonal relationships. On the contrary, setting healthy boundaries will allow you to have more authentic and satisfying relationships. As therapist Virginia Satir mentioned in "Peoplemaking" (1972), people grow and develop through our interactions with others. We need others to reflect who we are and to help us see and understand parts of ourselves that we might otherwise overlook.

But for these relationships to be healthy and allow us to grow, we need to have healthy boundaries. We need to know where we end and where the other begins. This not only protects us from emotional dependency, but also allows us to respect the autonomy of others.

And this is where another key skill we have discussed in this book comes into play: assertiveness. Assertiveness, as we learned in Chapter 13, is the ability to express our needs and desires in a way that respects both our rights and the rights of others. Through assertiveness, we can communicate our boundaries to others in a clear and respectful manner.

Let me give you an example. Suppose you have a friend who constantly asks you for favors, but is rarely available when you need help. Instead of allowing this situation to continue, which would cause resentment and damage your self-esteem, you could say something like, "I really value our friendship and am happy to help you when I can. However, I also need to feel that this relationship is reciprocal. I would like you to also be available to help me when I need it."

This is just one example, of course. Every situation is unique and will require a unique response. But the important thing is not to be afraid to express your needs and set boundaries. Remember, you are the gardener of your own mental garden. And while this work can be challenging, it can also be deeply rewarding.

Imagine how it would feel to have a garden full of flowers of self-esteem and trees of autonomy, a garden that reflects your growth and development as a person. Imagine how it would feel to know that you are the architect of this garden, that you are responsible for its beauty and balance.

This is the hope for change that I want you to keep in mind. The hope that you can break free from the chains of emotional dependency and cultivate a healthy, self-reliant future.

And here we come to the end of our journey, where we have explored every corner of the labyrinth of emotional dependence, and discovered together the treasures hidden in every curve, in every nook and cranny, and under every stone.

Have you noticed how your perception of the world, of yourself, has changed during this journey? Don't you feel stronger, more capable? More like a master gardener than a lost visitor in a wild, uncontrollable garden.

I want you to be proud of yourself for the courage and determination you have shown in facing your fears and challenges. You may still have things to learn and areas to grow in, but the journey of a thousand miles begins with one step, and you have already taken many of those steps.

This book may end here, but your journey continues. And I want you to know that you are not alone. Just as hikers help each other on a trail, all the people who have read this book, who have struggled and found the courage to grow, are by your side. We are a community, united by hope and the desire to change.

I feel fortunate to have been able to share this journey with you. It has been a real pleasure to accompany you on this journey, to show you the way and to see how you have grown in strength and understanding.

I want to thank you for joining me on this journey, for your courage and persistence. You are an inspiration and I am grateful to have had the opportunity to be a part of your journey.

And even though this book is coming to an end, I want you to know that this is not a goodbye. It is a "see you later", a "see you at the top". Because I know you will continue to grow, you will continue to learn, you will continue to free yourself from the chains of emotional dependency. And I'm excited to see the future that awaits you.

So, dear reader, my friend, thank you. Thank you for your courage, your determination, and your heart. I wish you the best on the road ahead. I wish you a future full of health, of autonomy, of self-love. A future in which you feel free and at peace.

See you at the summit, my friend. See you at the summit.

Farewell: The End of the Journey: A New Beginning Towards Emotional Freedom

Dear reader, dear friend, we have reached the end of this journey together, but really, this is just the beginning of a new path for you, one that is marked by self-knowledge, resilience and emotional independence.

We have explored together the intricate pathways of emotional dependency, its origins and how it manifests itself in our lives and relationships. We have discovered the crucial role that self-esteem plays in emotional dependency and how our culture and society can fuel it. But we have also learned that there is hope, that emotional dependency can be overcome, and that it is possible to build healthy relationships and an autonomous identity.

We have dismantled the myths about loneliness and learned to see it not as an enemy, but as an ally. We have discovered the importance of assertiveness and self-understanding and have seen how self-love can be the driving force behind emotional independence.

Now, you have in your hands the tools and knowledge you need to move forward on your path to emotional independence. But remember, this is a journey of continuous evolution and growth, and there will always be new things to learn and discover.

I would recommend that you continue to cultivate resilience and self-understanding, continue to practice assertiveness and self-care, and keep boundaries present in your relationships. And, of course, never lose sight of the hope for change and the desire for a healthy, self-reliant future.

I hope that what we have shared here has been useful to you and that it will lead you to find the freedom and happiness you deserve. May this book be the beginning of your path to emotional liberation and the start of a fuller and more autonomous life.

With all my love, I wish the best for you on your journey. May you find the peace, self-love and freedom you long for.

With love,

Antonio Jaimez.

One last favor

Dear

I hope you enjoyed reading my book. I would like to thank you for taking the time to read it and I hope you found value in its contents. I am writing to you today to make a very important request.

As an independent author, reviews are extremely valuable to me. Not only do they help me get valuable feedback on my work, but they can also influence other readers' decision to buy the book. If you could take a few minutes to leave an honest review on Amazon, it would be a great help to me.

Again, I thank you for taking the time to read my book and for considering my review request. Your feedback and support means a lot to me as an independent author.

You can also find more books on this subject from my Amazon author page.

https://www.amazon.es/~/e/B0C4TS75MD

You can also visit my website <u>www.libreriaonlinemax.com</u> where you will find all kinds of hypnosis explained in detail, hypnotherapies, free resources and expert level courses. You can also use the following QR code:

Best regards,

Antonio Jaimez

Printed in Great Britain
by Amazon